What's Your
BRIDAL
Style?

What's Your BRIDAL Style?

SHARON NAYLOR

AND

CASEY COOPER
Botanicals, Inc.

CITADEL PRESS
Kensington Publishing Corp.
www.kensingtonbooks.com

CITADEL PRESS BOOKS are published by

Kensington Publishing Corp.
850 Third Avenue
New York, NY 10022

All Kensington titles, imprints, and distributed lines are available at special
quantity discounts for bulk purchases for sales promotions, premiums, fund-
raising, educational, or institutional use. Special book excerpts or customized
printings can also be created to fit specific needs. For details, write or phone the
office of the Kensington special sales manager: Kensington Publishing Corp.,
850 Third Avenue, New York, NY 10022, attn: Special Sales Department;
phone 1-800-221-2647.

CITADEL PRESS and the Citadel logo are Reg. U.S. Pat. & TM Off.

First printing: October 2007

10 9 8 7 6 5 4 3 2 1

Printed in the United States of America

Library of Congress Control Number: 2007929062

ISBN-13: 978-0-8065-2829-8
ISBN-10: 0-8065-2829-X

To my husband, John, who is just my style.
—CC

To Madison and Kevin
—SN

Contents

Introduction

Vowing to spend the rest of your life with another person is an extraordinary thing to celebrate.

Once upon a time, there were many rules attached to a wedding celebration. There were expectations of what a wedding should look like and feel like. There was structure. There was form. Nowadays the expectation is that the style of a wedding celebration is a direct reflection of the bride and groom's personalities. *You're* making up the rules. *You're* finding the form. You and your chosen life partner have the freedom to create an event you imagine suits your style

What is *your* bridal style?

You may have a vision . . . a formal ballroom with a crystal chandelier . . . or a flower-filled garden . . . or a barefoot beach wedding. Your imagination is giving you snapshots of the setting, the wedding cake, the first dance, little glimpses of your day— some vivid and some blurry. But when a wedding vendor is sitting there before you with a clipboard and a blank piece of paper, asking you to describe your *style*, you can't quite put the images into words. He or she may throw phrases at you: "Would you describe your style as city-chic? Whimsical? Tuscan-inspired?" The words flutter around your head like butterflies. What exactly does Tuscan-inspired *mean?*

When you are able to *define* your wedding style, it will be much easier and certainly more productive when communicating with the experts you've hired to help you create the wedding of your dreams. Your wedding experts stand ready to bring your *unique* vision to life. But they're not mind-readers. The dialogue, the *adjectives*, phrases, colors, textures, scents, tastes, sounds, and any visuals you bring into a meeting to help your vendors understand you and your fiancé will act as a launching pad for the creative process. Any wedding expert worth their salt will certainly spend the time drawing information out of their clients. But, you're looking at a process that lasts a mere one to two hours and typically plays into their specific expertise: flowers, food, music. Working with a client who has spent more than one to two hours exploring their style and is able to describe it translates into a much more cohesive event that is a direct reflection of *YOU*.

This is the *new* first step in wedding planning, the definition of your bridal style. We're going to help you describe your wedding into existence. You bring every image in your mind into this work, and we'll give you the words and the tools to communicate to each and every one of your vendors the *essence* of what you want. Once they understand the essence of your style, they can take it from there and completely wow you with the results of their interpretation of your style. We'll teach you how to take His Style and marry it with Your Style. We'll teach you to go *beyond* what you see in the bridal magazines. We'll teach you how to define your style when you may not even know what it is yourself.

Your celebration should, ideally, reflect your style as a couple.

How do you take two completely separate individuals with two completely different histories and two completely different sets of influences, often resulting in two completely different styles, and *marry* them? What if I'm city-chic and he's down-home Southern? or some variation of a seemingly oil-and-water preference clash. We promise you . . . we will guide you to a style definition that will blend the two styles beautifully.

It takes a bit of work at the beginning. But, if you both commit to participating in the process of defining your style at the start of your life together, the results will be lasting. This is a priceless perk of using this book. As you work through the intake questionnaire, your answers will certainly apply to your wedding, but they'll also reach beyond the wedding. Think of all of the decisions couples make together that are influenced by personal style: deciding on the furniture arrangement in the living room, picking paint colors, purchasing homes, buying cars, selecting names for children, deciding where to retire. If your styles differ, or if you haven't spent much time thinking about or defining your style, or, for that matter, finding out much about your fiance's style, these types of decisions can be a real struggle. We believe that defining your style—and marrying each of your individual styles—helps you now, and delivers lasting returns for your investment of time.

The work proposed in Chapter One will help you to plan your celebration in such a way that personifies and celebrates each of you as individuals, as well as personifying and celebrating the two of you as a couple. The goal of the questions you find in the upcoming pages is to stimulate your imagination and your senses. Make dates with each other to sit down with this book. Allow a little bit of "marinating time" for your answers to age and expand. Time, and imagination, are the way to experience this process. Enjoy it.

Do not expect to agree on everything. Express your ideas, opinions, and desires. Reveal. Discover. Argue. Explore. Push. Push back. Listen. Struggle. Compromise. This is the stuff marriages are made of. Of course, sometimes there is no compromise. When you cannot find one, take turns. When there isn't a natural compromise, both of you need to really tune in and be honest about which one of you the result of the decision matters to the most. We will guide you over some of the stumbling blocks. We know from experience that not everything blends easily, and that maybe the beauty will exist side-by-side. Your bridal style will inform your partnering style. During an engagement, any insight into your partnering style is a true gift.

If you're feeling a little overwhelmed right now, that's completely normal. It's an enormous undertaking not only to define your overall wedding style, but to define your style in *each area* of the wedding plans (like your music, your menu, your favors, and your wardrobe). But don't worry. This new first step in wedding planning is designed to make the entire process *easier* as you go along. You'll see that it builds upon itself. Each of the questions you answer in chapter 1 corresponds throughout the book, giving you a strong foundation, and then we'll delve further into each additional detail of your wedding.

So start with chapter 1. Answer each of the intake questions. Do the exercises and take notes. And then go right to your highest priority chapter, like the wedding gown or the flowers, the menu or the photography. You make your own process, plan in your own order, after chapter 1. Still have questions? We encourage you to visit our Web sites to see the images we've posted on our "What's Your Bridal Style?" pages. The graphics we've collected just might enhance your process even further.

We're thrilled to guide you, so let's get started on defining your bridal style . . .

Acknowledgments

We couldn't have created this book without the open-arms enthusiasm of our editor Danielle Chiotti at Citadel Press and our agent, the great Meredith Bernstein. We're overjoyed to work with you.

A very special thank-you as well to the many experts and luminaries who graciously provided their time and wisdom: Sasha Souza; Randie Pellegrini; Dominique Schurman of Papyrus; Michelle Roth; Henry Roth; Patty Brahe of mountaincow.com; Kristy Nuttall at mylittlepretty.com; Stacey Koerner of beautyon call.com; Rita Gutekanst of Limelight Catering; John Rudy of Catering Resources; Neille Hoffman of Aurum Design; Andrew Ettenhofer of Fig Media; Richard Milne of Rank Entertainment; Michele Wolff of the Family Institute at Northwestern University; Reverend Laurie Sue Brockway; and Rachel Clementi of Hearts on Fire. We adore you all for your style and your generosity of spirit.

PART ONE

Setting Your Foundation

CHAPTER 1

Exploring Your Style

In order to be active participants in designing your wedding, you need to develop a vision and acquire the necessary tools for communicating that vision to all your vendors. No, you do not have to have your vision fully fleshed out right away. It will take time and effort, and the input of your pros. After all, you will select talented and artistic vendors to help you realize and contribute to your vision along the way.

What's essential right now is defining your sense of personal style, and that's where you'll begin.

The wedding team you hire will need to know as much as possible about who you are as a couple and what type of essence you want to achieve on your wedding day. So you'll use the upcoming questions and exercises to fully express your personalities, your favorite things, and even your individual style differences, as well as outline your vision for your wedding day.

After you work through this chapter, the additional chapters offer more specific details to further refine your style in everything from the invitations to your apparel; to the type and length of the ceremony; to the photography, flowers, food, and music;

3

and more. Think of each choice you make as a spice, and all the spices will blend to create an overall flavor.

Defining your personal style hinges on the five senses, so you will soon be asked to explore your favorites in each of these areas, as they tap right into your emotions and influence most of the choices you make in your daily life. For instance, think about your fiancé in relation to the five senses. You might think, I fell in love with my fiancé because I like how tall he is and I love the way his hair feels and I could listen to the sound of his voice for the rest of my life.

The tasks in this chapter might seem involved, but you and your soon-to-be will have fun working on them together. If you have a reluctant partner, or you're both very pressed for time, plan several mini-dates when you'll work on the questions. This will help you discuss important issues for the wedding day, and help you connect with *each other*—a task that may become surprisingly difficult in the months leading up to the wedding. *If you make the time now, it will save you time in the future.* So plan a casual evening; order a pizza, grab a six-pack of beer or a bottle of Chianti, and dedicate a couple of hours to this project.

Step 1: Develop Your Possibilities Notebook

Your Possibilities Notebook will be an organized binder containing hundreds of pictures and descriptions, color samples, swatches, magazine ads, and more . . . all of the things that strike you as possible inspirations for your day. Use a simple three-ring binder and a slew of clear plastic sleeves, plenty of loose-leaf paper, and folders with pockets where you'll insert clippings and other surprising items (such as a pumpkin-colored paper napkin from a kid's birthday party that perfectly captures the color palette you want for your fall wedding). From ads to photos to color and fabric swatches, even greeting cards and catalog covers, you'll collect a wealth of visual and tactile items to inform your bridal style. (Visit our websites, www.sharonnaylor.net and www.botanicalschicago.com for a detailed list of inspiring possibilities in each category of your wedding plans.)

You'll keep this Possibilities Notebook handy, such as in your car for easy access, and you'll bring it with you when you meet with each of your wedding vendors. This way, you can flip open to the invitations section and pull out that orange paper napkin to show your designer exactly the color of accent you want on your ecru cards. You'll be adding information to this notebook throughout the wedding planning process, and the plastic sleeves will allow you to easily add and remove images and clippings as needed.

You can categorize your Possibilities Notebook any way you like, but if you're looking for a template, separating it into Likes, Dislikes, His, Hers, Ours is a good place to start. And, if you have very helpful parents and friends, you can create a section for their input, but *only* if you find it useful.

To get started creating your Possibilities Notebook, plan an initial date and time, knowing that it will take two to three hours to make some great headway. Then, start filling each section with images that jump out at you from at least six different magazines or catalogs: fashion, bridal, music, interior décor, home, gardening, auto, outdoor, travel, celebrity, to name a few. Select publications that play into your collective interests. Go through and tear out every page that appeals to you for *any* reason. (On the flip side, it is extremely useful to pull a pile of images that you absolutely hate. You learn almost as much about your style acknowledging things you *don't* like.) This will be the start of a journal that helps to shape and integrate your style now and in the future. You'll continue pulling and filing photos and magazine clippings throughout your wedding-planning months. You never know when a gorgeous magazine cover will inspire something for the wedding, or perhaps for your future home!

The images you pull can range wildly: a faucet, the color of a wall, a tree in full flower, a handbag, a chunk of chocolate, a glass of merlot, a car, a flat screen computer monitor, a Victorian home, the dress Charlize Theron wore to the Oscars . . . all these visuals will stimulate your mind and get you thinking visually and emotionally. Every single image will reveal something about who you are.

Perhaps the best thing about the Possibilities Notebook is that you'll be able to use it again later for nonwedding events. If you ever meet with an architect or interior designer, when you're picking out fabric for new drapes, when you select a gift for your spouse on your first anniversary, flip through this collection of images.

You will learn so much about each other's personal tastes and style, and as you know in your relationship, it takes trust and honesty to reveal your inner thoughts and beliefs. So as you work together on this notebook, or when you both reveal to each other your own independent additions to it, treat this process with *personal* care. Be respectful of each other's choices, don't censor yourself or your partner, and don't make fun of one another if you don't agree with an image or think a color pairing looks gaudy. Give each other total freedom, and keep the partnership aspect of your Possibilities Notebook in mind as you work through the questions in this book. Here, too, you'll be revealing aspects of your personality, and there are no right or wrong answers. So right at the start of this process, assure one another that "Your choices are safe with me." When your partner knows that he's not going to be judged for his input, he's going to open up. And so are you.

You could complete the entire notebook in a day, or you could take your time working on it together, taking weeks to work on one section at a time. Whatever fits your schedules best without rushing. No matter how long you take at your own pace, give yourselves the best advantage by having enough examples and inspirations to show your experts. One fabric swatch might be enough to show your gown designer, but you might have thirty photos of updos to show your hairstylist.

Step 2: The Bridal Questionnaire

The second step is to answer the questions in the Bridal Questionnaire. Plan another date with your fiancé, whether it's a cozy afternoon by the fire or a lovely dinner by candlelight. If you're really pressed for time, a lengthy car trip would be an excellent time to work on this questionnaire. Yes, this is a long questionnaire and it can be overwhelming to see *so* many questions stretching for so many pages. It's specifically designed to be detailed like this, so that you'll bring out your best keywords. Given its length, feel free to schedule a few sessions with one another—

just like with your Possibilities Notebook—perhaps doing one section a day so that you're both fresh and in the mood to participate fully. And like the Possibilities Notebook, you can come back to these questions and plug in new entries as time goes on.

Wherever and whenever you take the quiz, the most important thing is that you're both present and involved in the process whenever you work on it together. As you each answer these questions, put your answers in writing. Also jot down keywords and phrases in the margins of this book as you go along, which will allow you to refer back to your initial answers as the planning process moves forward. Months from now when things get stressful, you'll appreciate having your original engaged-bliss ideas and phrases.

Now, in terms of finances, we're not all exactly where we want to be in life. So, many of these questions involve how things are now, how you would like them to be in your future, and finally, what they would be if money were no object. So, again, don't censor yourselves with a "we can't afford chair linens, so we won't even think about it," because you never know what freebies you might find in the future. Open yourselves to *everything* possible as you brainstorm your answers here.

An Overview of Your Style (You will see this again later)

- Bride: Describe your sense of personal style, such as "I'm conservative," or "I'm quirky and artsy." (No need to limit yourself to one word; you may embody lots of different styles depending on your moods.)
- Groom: Describe your sense of personal style.

❧ Describe each other's personal style as you see it.
(This question is quite revealing! It's often very fun to see
the positive ways your partner "reads" you, the descriptions
you never knew he/she would use to describe you.)

Home

❧ When you walk through your home, what colors and
textures and lines do you see?
❧ What kind of decorative items, knickknacks, and art do
you own?
❧ What types of fabric do you gravitate toward when
decorating (upholstery, rugs, pillows, drapes, etc.)?
❧ What is the quintessential aspect of your home that gives
it that homey feeling?
❧ If you live with your fiancé, how did you blend your styles
into a home that suits the both of you? How did you decide
which couch made the cut and which coffee table went to
Goodwill?
❧ If money were no object, what would you see when you
walk through your home?

Fashion

❧ When you open your closet, what colors do you see?
❧ What types of fabric do you prefer to wear?
❧ What designer labels make you feel the best? Why?
❧ Describe the outfit in your wardrobe that makes you feel
the most like yourself, the outfit you would wear every day
if you thought no one would notice.

* Describe the outfit in your wardrobe that makes you feel the most beautiful or handsome.
* When you think of your future spouse, which outfit or apparel style reflects that individual the most?
* Describe your tie collection, if you have one.
* Describe your lingerie or boxer/brief apparel.
* Describe your shoe collection, or shoe assortment, if it doesn't quite rate as a collection.
* If money were no object, what would be your fantasy wardrobe?
* What items do you most enjoy shopping for? Why?
* Do you wear jewelry? If so, which items?

Use the next four questions as your style definition guide for your wedding rings as well as an important quality for your overall wedding style. The amount of sparkle you like in your jewelry could illustrate the amount of sparkle for your day.

---

* Do you prefer gold, silver, white gold, or platinum?
* What precious stones are you drawn to? Why?
* Where do you shop for your jewelry?
* Where would you like to shop for your jewelry?
* Which fashion magazines and catalogs do you read?
* Describe how your fashion sense reflects your personality.
* Do you have a fashion sense as a couple? (i.e., power couple in business suits; crunchy couple in Birkenstocks) or do you and your partner mismatch? (i.e., he's in preppie gear and you're in grunge).

Personal Appearance

- Do you have long hair or short hair? Why?
- How much money are you willing to pay for a haircut?
- Do you color your hair? Why? If you do color your hair, what color(s) do you gravitate toward?
- If you color your hair, do you do it yourself or have it done professionally?
- Do you wear makeup? If so, what brand(s) of makeup and skin care products do you purchase?
- Do you manicure and pedicure? If so, do you do it yourself or have it done professionally?
- Do you wear a color on your fingernails or toenails? Why? If you do paint your fingernails or toenails, what color(s) do you gravitate toward?
- Which aspects of your personal appearance most reflect *you*?
- Which aspects of your future spouse's personal appearance most reflect *him* or *her*?

Career

- Where do you work?
- If you have a title, what is it?
- What does your job entail on a mental level each day?
- What does your job entail on a physical level each day?
- What do you like most about your job?
- What do you like the least about your job?
- How do you feel when you tell someone what you do for a living?

- What is your dream job and why?
- How do your career paths frame you and your future spouse as a couple?

Transportation

- What method(s) do you use for transportation? Do you use this method due to choice or necessity?
- What is your *preferred* method of transportation?
- How does your mode of transportation reflect your personality?
- Describe your driving style. How is it reflected in your everyday life? (i.e., cautious, aggressive, halting)
- What make and model of car or cars do you drive?
- What colors appear throughout the car on the inside and outside?
- What fabrics and materials appear throughout the car on the inside and outside?
- When you get a new car, what will you purchase?
- How often do you wash your car?
- Do you wash it yourself or take it to a carwash?
- If money were no object, describe the car of your dreams. How would you feel behind the wheel of this car?

Taste Buds

- What is your favorite meal? (include appetizer, beverage, main course, side dishes, and dessert). Describe the appeal of these foods as they relate to all five senses.
- If you chew gum, what flavor of gum do you like to chew?

- If you eat candy, what is your favorite candy?
- What fruits do you like?
- What vegetables do you like?
- Do you like seafood? If so, what kind?
- Do you like meat? If so, what kind?
- What is your favorite nonalcoholic beverage?
- If you drink, what is your favorite alcoholic beverage?
- What is your favorite special occasion drink? What makes that drink feel celebratory?
- If you drink coffee, how do you take it?
- Pick a spice that would be most reflective of *you*.
- Which cuisine best describes the flavor of your relationship?

Scents

- Do you wear perfume or cologne? Why or why not?
- What scents do you look for in a perfume or cologne for yourself?
- What scents to do you look for in a perfume or cologne for your partner?
- Name the fragrances of your shampoo, body lotion, and deodorant.
- What is your favorite aroma related to food?
- What is your least favorite aroma related to food?
- Discuss the three most pleasant smells that immediately come to mind.
- Discuss the three most unpleasant smells that immediately come to mind.

Sound

- What types of sounds encourage you to feel peaceful and calm?
- What sounds give you the shivers?
- What sounds set you on edge or startle you?
- List three people you know or know of with really distinctive voices. What do you like or dislike about the quality of their voice?
- What is your first memory of music?
- Do you play one or more musical instruments? If not, what musical instrument would you want to play?
- What is the musical instrument that you feel most attached to, either listening to or playing?
- What types of music do you purchase?
- What radio stations do you listen to? Why?
- Do you enjoy attending live concerts? Why? What are the last few concerts you've attended?
- If there was a soundtrack playing in the background of your entire love story, name songs, musicians, or a types of music that would be on that soundtrack.

Touch

- Describe your favorite comfort items and how they feel.
- Describe your bedding, mattress, pillows, sheets, blankets, and comforter.
- Name several items that you find repulsive to touch.
- Name several items you find irresistible to touch.
- Name several items that are sensitive to your touch.

- How would you describe the feeling of your favorite part of your partner's body? Of your body?
- What type(s) of shoes do you wear? Socks? Tights? Hose? How do they make you feel?
- What types of surfaces do you enjoy walking on with bare feet?
- When you get into a body of water, do you jump in all at once, or work your way in bit by bit? What temperature do you prefer the water to be? Name your favorite type of water to swim in and why.

Your Favorite Things

- List your three favorite colors.
- List your three least favorite colors.
- List three of your favorite gifts to give.
- List three of your favorite gifts to receive.
- Where is your favorite place to spend your free time?
- What is your favorite room in the house and why?
- What are your three favorite buildings in the world?
- Name your three most admired artists.
- List your three favorite authors.
- What are your three favorite musical artists of all time?
- List your three favorite movies of all time.
- What is your favorite holiday?

Additional Questions

- Describe yourself in the first five to ten adjectives that come into your head.

- Describe your partner in the first five to ten adjectives that come into your head.
- What are your current hobbies?
- What types of hobbies would you like to explore?
- If you like animals, name the types of animals you like.
- Do you have pets? Why or why not?
- If you won the lottery, name the first three things you would do.
- What is your vision of a perfect day?
- Are you a spiritual person? If so, how? If not, how?

Now that you've worked through these questions, getting really detailed with your answers and really thinking about the many facets of your likes and dislikes, answer the first two questions again to see if you have more clarity in your sense of style:

- Bride: Describe your personal style.
- Groom: Describe your personal style.
- Describe each other's sense of style.

You might find that you *thought* you were conservative, but you actually have a yearning for something flashy, such as a shiny silver convertible car or hot red stilettos. That's going to figure beautifully into your wedding plans, when you mix classic flowers, food, and music with sensual red silk table linens. Or if you've discovered that you're classic but eco-friendly, that may translate into a more natural-colored tableau, or even the location of your wedding in a botanical garden with invitations printed on pretty recycled paper and organic food on your menu . . . something you never thought of before.

You might be swimming in details right now, but know that you're on your way! You've just accomplished a very important part of your wedding plans. Many of the key phrases and words you'll use to define your bridal style throughout the planning process *are already written down*. They've been waiting to be discovered, to come play a part of your wedding day, and you connected with them when you answered the questionnaire.

Now, for each of the questions on the previous pages, go back and circle the keywords that jump out at you. This will take you to the next step in using these words to create your style definition *or*—and this is very important in our era of style blending and personalization—using these words to blend two or more different styles. The work you've just completed with this questionnaire will be utilized throughout the book as you delve into the world of wedding wardrobes, reception menus, wedding day transportation, and the like. There will be additional questions throughout the chapters that relate *specifically* to your style as it applies to each chapter title.

Which words did you write down most often?

Step 3: Building Your Bridal-Style Vocabulary

The focus of this section is to get you dreaming *and experiencing* what you'd love to create for your wedding *before getting into the planning process*. Again, while you may have thought of your style as *romantic* before starting on this book, by the end of the process, you'll see that romantic has many more facets and textures and colors and lines.

Below is a list of some style categories along with several free-associated descriptive words. The process of elimination is an integral part of defining your bridal style, after all, so if a style doesn't attract you at all, cross it off. For those categories that entice you, we've left you space to fill in words, memories, adjectives, and sensorial associations that come to mind when you think of those styles. As you explore the list, you may be surprised to find that *exotic* is calling to you, or that *organic* is right up your alley, or maybe both! When two or more categories attract your attention, the layering of styles generates exceptional and original ideas, so we're starting you off with a collection of image-inspiring words.

Adventurous
- thrilling
- risky
- daring
- gutsy
- bold
- unabashed

Architectural
- structural
- engineered
- purposeful surfaces
- linear
- Escher drawings
- Frank Lloyd Wright
- skyscrapers

Arts and Crafts
- craftsmanship
- simple lines and shapes
- William Morris
- mission
- stained glass
- beautiful wood

Bohemian

- beatnik
- nomadic
- artistic
- free-flowing
- unconventional

Classic

- timeless
- definitive
- quintessential
- archetypal
- legendary

City Chic

- martinis
- skyscrapers
- bustling night life
- Jimmy Choo shoes
- fashionable
- *Sex and the City*
- melting pot

Contemporary

- trendy
- cutting edge
- modern
- in vogue
- new-fangled
- current

Country Club Chic

- pearls
- tennis whites
- nautical
- oversized designer sunglasses
- exclusive
- year-round tan
- diamond tennis bracelets

Eclectic

- diverse
- assorted
- layered
- surprising
- mixing and matching a variety of periods and styles
- bohemian
- gypsy

Elegant

- graceful
- flowing sheer fabric
- classical music

- coordinated details
- chic
- classy

Exotic

- mysterious
- imported
- adventurous
- rare
- indulgent
- fiery
- tangy
- unfamiliar
- striking

Fairy Tale

- enchanted
- magical
- imaginative
- myth
- princess gown
- *Lord of the Rings*
- unicorns

Glamorous or Glam

- gorgeous
- sexy
- alluring

- feather boas
- false eyelashes
- glittery
- extravagant

Graphic

- strong contrast of shape and color
- explicit
- striking
- vivid
- sharp
- geometric
- bold

Minimalist

- pure
- unembellished
- spare
- sleek
- modern
- stark

Organic

- earthy
- natural
- healthy
- fresh

- textural
- roots
- bark
- green (more than just a color, but a movement, as well)

Preppy

- Ralph Lauren
- monograms
- boarding school
- summer at the Cape
- sailing
- proper etiquette
- traditional

Romantic

- Merchant Ivory
- candlelight
- champagne
- mythic
- violins
- lyrical
- fairy tale

Shabby Chic

- overstuffed
- comfortable

- flowery
- rumpled elegance
- pleats and ruffles
- worn, faded, distressed
- soft

Sophisticated

- red lipstick
- little black dress
- designer
- worldly
- cosmopolitan
- polished
- caviar

Tailored

- sophisticated
- linear
- custom
- Ann Taylor
- clean
- precise
- unfussy
- pressed

Traditional

- ritual
- established

* time-honored
* "By the Book"
* customary
* habitual

Trendy

* hip
* hot
* popular
* "Tony"

Understated

* simple
* modest
* minimalist
* unpretentious
* low-key
* quiet

Whimsical

* fanciful
* quirky
* capricious
* bright
* unexpected
* playful

Zen

* sand
* the four elements: Wind, Water, Wood, and Fire
* wind chimes
* serenity
* earth tones
* breath
* running water

Concentrate on the style categories that appeal to you, then in your Possibilities Notebook write down twenty or more reactions or thoughts that are inspired by each style you like. And if there is a style you love, such as Moroccan or Asian or 1920s flapper style, don't be afraid to start your own list. Free-associate the images from those regions or eras you love, and keep these styles in mind as you move into the next chapter on color.

CHAPTER 2

Color

What colors inspire you?
Do you stop in your tracks when you see the sunset filling the sky with a palette of indigo, violet, and pink? Do you dream of the azure ocean in the Caribbean? Salivate over the thought of a fresh, juicy mango? Pull out your wallet at the first sight of a bright yellow gerbera daisy in a florist's window? Take a deep, relaxed breath as you watch the light color of the cream swirl into the rich chocolate brown of your cup of morning coffee? The colors that *move* you could very well paint your wedding's style.

LOOK AROUND

Once you start looking, you'll realize that color is all around you. Even a display of men's neckties can be a fabulous color inspiration! Also, check out the Pantone color sample pack sold through www.hgtv.com. It's a collection of colored strips that interior designers use to plan the hues of their project rooms.

Your wedding day is a combination of several mini-events. The ceremony, the cocktail hour, the wedding reception, even the after-party can be treated as individual events in terms of color palette. You are welcome to tell your story and express your couple style throughout each of these events. By creating separate personalities and palettes for each event, you put your individual stamp on your wedding, keeping it unique and personalized, as well as stimulating for your guests.

Even if you think you already know your wedding's color scheme (your bridesmaids will wear celery green, for example), this section will *still* guide and inspire you. After all, every part of your wedding day is colorful. You have a choice about most of the colors that will be part of your day: the food, the flowers, the martinis on the drink menu, your method of transportation, the ink on your place cards, your linen, and the frosting on your cake, to name just a few. And every color will move you in a different way.

What we're working toward in this chapter is associating the *words* and *feelings* inspired by color. It may be that eggplant purple never entered your mind as part of your wedding color scheme, but once you've explored how it makes you feel, you're reminded of a Sunday spent in your grandmother's garden when you were a child. Perhaps you followed behind as she pulled ripe eggplants from the ground, and relished the aroma in her kitchen when she fried and layered the eggplant circles for a parmigiana. Just that rich, deep color brings back a memory, a feeling, an aroma, a taste . . . these kinds of senses conjured up by color will play into defining so much of your wedding weekend style. So, even if you have chosen celery green dresses for your bridesmaids, you may be drawn to a gorgeous array of eggplant miniature calla lilies for their bouquets. An unexpected and beautiful color combination inspired by your sense memory.

Your favorite shoes. What color are they? What is it about wearing that color that makes you feel ready for a night on the town? What is it about that color of shoes that makes you feel sexy and seductive, or elegant and sophisticated?

What color are your favorite sheets? Your favorite towels? What color do you wrap yourself in every day?

SASHA SOUZA'S COLOR CHART

Celebrity wedding coordinator Sasha Souza has a fabulous feature on her website (www.sashasouzaevents.com). Since she is known throughout the world as "the designer who loves color," she has created on her Art of Wedding Design page an interactive tool where you can click on the square showing your favorite color, and your choice reveals an insight about you. For instance, part of the revelation for the color teal is "Optimistic and trusting, you have a high degree of faith and hope, easily trusting others." Each of you will select the color that's most attractive to you, and you'll both find out what that color reveals.

Color is unbelievably subjective. When communicating your thoughts on color to your vendors, being able to match a color with an *emotion* or *experience* gets your message across on a higher level. For instance, when talking with your florist, you might say that you'd like the flowers at the cocktail party to convey a sense of expectation, like a freshly halved summertime cantaloupe that's waiting to be sliced and eaten. The florist will glean a great deal of information from a statement like that, not only about color but also about fragrance, texture, and emotion. Given such a statement, the florist might design the cocktail party floral as the beginning of the design story of your wedding, creating pieces with a combination of cantaloupe tones mixed perhaps with a touch of pink to complement the central color. Splashes of light green might be included in these small but exquisite arrangements, emulating the green of the cantaloupe rind. Or, you could use a partially hollowed out cantaloupe half nestled in a bed of coral and blush rose petals and filled with a bit of water and topped with a floating candle. The possibilities are endless.

Below you'll see we've listed a small range of colors, and we'd like you to write down the words, feelings, and experiences that come to mind. Don't stop at our list, though. Pick up your favorite scarf and use that color. Use paint chips from the home improvement store. Choose the ones that catch your eye or move you in some way, and then write your inspiration words on those. Insert them into your Possibilities Notebook and bring them to your wedding experts for a meaning-filled example of the hues and tones that you connect with.

Color	Bride's Words	Groom's Words
red		
crimson		
magenta		
fuchsia		

Color	Bride's Words	Groom's Words
rose		
blush		
coral		
salmon		
apricot		
mango		
copper		
burnt sienna		
amber		
lemon		
chartreuse		
jade		
sage		
moss		
forest		
indigo		
turquoise		
ultramarine		

Color	Bride's Words	Groom's Words
violetblush		
lavender		
eggplant		
coffee		
chocolate		
charcoal		
ebony		
white		
cream		
sand		

The name we attach to a color speaks volumes. Have you ever had the experience of being swayed by a paint sample, not because of the actual color you were seeing, but, because of the name: Freshly Squeezed Lemons; New England Mist; Zinc . . . ? Or have you ever found yourself ordering a baby blue cashmere sweater, even though you don't like baby blue, because the catalog called it Lake, and that sounded so appealing? The name of the color taps directly into your emotional response to it.

Fill in your own colors here: _____

STYLE NOTES

Need some more inspiration in color? Visit www.sessions. edu/ilu/, the interactive color wheel that allows you to combine tones, play with the shading, see the pairings right there on the screen, then e-mail them to your vendors or print them out for a far better expression than if you if you just said, "blue and green."

CHAPTER 3

The Four Seasons

Do you have a favorite time of year? A season you look forward to so much you can almost taste it? This chapter explores the decision that will create the foundation of all your other wedding day details—the season of your wedding date. You will determine this by writing down sounds, scenery, tastes, smells, and favorite memories that you associate with the four seasons. By choosing a date that coincides with your favorite season, you'll have endless opportunities to layer your event with seasonal influences.

If for some reason you can't book your wedding during the season of your dreams, you can create a fragrant springtime wedding in the middle of February with the use of color and flowers and lighting. If summer is your cup of tea, but you're getting married in the fall, take an element from summer that you love and tweak it. For example, if you love ice cream cones on a hot summer night, have the caterer pass out petite sorbet ice cream cones during dancing, but incorporate fall colors and flavors with the sorbet: pomegranate, coffee, or fig. The opportunities for *nuance* throughout your wedding are limitless.

Below are some examples for each season, but it is important that you and your fiancé explore your own influences and history in how you relate to them. Much like the work in chapter 2 with color, the emotional and sensory associations you make give your design team a big advantage in fulfilling your vision. Jot down the words that leap to mind when you think about crisp spring mornings or silent winter midnights, loud family holiday dinners, what autumn football season smells like . . . and then think about how those images can translate into décor or theme ideas for your wedding.

Spring

(The bright green shoots of the daffodils poking through the drab brown mulch inspire you to use daffodils as the perfect accent to a chocolate brown linen theme; light blue Cadbury Easter egg candies inspire the color of the piping on the cake, and the color of the ink on the place cards and menu cards; the fragrance of lily of the valley and lilac inspire your bouquet choices.)

Image	*How You Can Incorporate It*
1.	
2.	
3.	
4.	
5.	

Summer

(The sights, smells, and tastes of summer could inspire the follow-ing types of wedding style notes: the Beach Boys music you al-ways loved at the beach could play for your cocktail party; driving with the top down translates into hiring a convertible instead of a limo; a frozen strawberry margarita is perfect for your bar card.)

Image	*How You Can Incorporate It*
1.	_____
2.	_____
3.	_____
4.	_____
5.	_____

Autumn

(Autumn might mean "football season" to you, so think about the elements of the season. The smell of barbecue translates to food choices for your rehearsal dinner or cocktail party; the bright burgundy color of the Japanese maple tree in your parents' front yard brings a rich burgundy palette into your wedding color scheme; hot apple cider joins your creative choices for after-dinner drinks; pomegranates become an accent to your entrees.)

Image	*How You Can Incorporate It*

1. _____

2. _____

3. _____

4. _____

5. _____

Winter

(Enormous snowflakes at the start of a big snowfall could be the graphic for your invitations; sitting by the fireplace inspires you to have the wedding at a site that has a fireplace for ambience; hot chocolate with whipped cream can be added to the dessert bar; pink Victorian Christmas ornaments could become centerpiece items; the church choir singing at candlelight mass could become a part of your ceremony.)

Image	*How You Can Incorporate It*

1. _____

2. _____

3. _____

4. _____

5. _____

Of course, within these images you'll undoubtedly have lots of sense memories, such as the feel of the first warm breeze of summertime. In the next chapter, you'll put your five senses to work in a broader way.

CHAPTER 4

The Five Senses

Sight, sound, taste, touch, and smell. You live every day with the tools to describe your bridal style. You just need to give them a little bit of time and thought. You've already accomplished a tremendous amount in the first three chapters. The information you are culling through all of these exercises will serve you in communicating with your vendors, as well as each other. You will be able to illustrate your wedding vision with a sensory description that allows the expert—and, in the future, your guests—to *experience* your wedding day.

This chapter explores each of the five senses, the emotions they evoke, memories associated with them, your favorite things—all play an enormous part of defining your bridal style. For instance, if you know the scent of lavender evokes a slew of positive emotions and/or experiences in your life, perhaps you'll incorporate lavender into your bouquet or your centerpieces, or give away lavender sachets as favors. If the sound of a babbling brook relaxes you and offers you an "escape" from your everyday life, you might choose a location that features a brook or waterfall on the grounds, or rent a venue that has a fountain.

Your response to the five senses stimulates memories. Your memories influence who you are today, now, in this moment, in this engagement, in this wedding, in this marriage. As you work through the following sections, write down the images that come to mind. Also, personalize this process by writing down your own keywords for your partner to respond to. For instance, you might write down, "sweet tastes," and see what he or she has to say. They might respond with Mounds bars and Creamsicles, which you now know to bring into your wedding plans as a Mounds-flavored martini and Creamsicle-flavored buttercream frosting for the petit fours. All from a simple sense exercise.

This is a broad, stream-of-consciousness exercise. You'll find, having done related work in the past few chapters, that there will be themes and ideas and memories that recur throughout this book. The recurring themes are what you're looking for, as these are the themes that will shape your wedding day. Be as specific as possible as you write these down, and provide context, when possible. The more specific you are, the clearer your memory of this sensorial experience becomes.

Sight

(A satisfying blue and purple sunset; stark, bare tree branches crystallized by ice during a winter storm and catching the sunlight during the thaw; a dense field of brightly colored red and yellow tulips; the speckled blue of robin's eggs protected by the brown twiggy nest; the charm of a summer cottage with fragrant rose arbors around the porch; the pastel blue and pink of sticky, sweet cotton candy; the clear and innocent blue eyes of an infant;

the graceful, gauzy flow of white organza curtains blowing in a light breeze.)

What are the beautiful sights you've seen that still make an impact on you now?

Bride   *Groom*

1. _____

2. _____

3. _____

4. _____

5. _____

What are some sight images you're imagining for your wedding?

Bride   *Groom*

1. _____

2. _____

3. _____

4. _____

5. _____

SHAPES AND PATTERNS

The sense of sight reveals shapes and patterns that may speak to you. So assess your feelings about square tables, long rectangular tables, a round bouquet to match your round engagement ring stone, a wedding cake made of square layers, oversized polka dots, Burberry striped patterns, heart shapes, etc. Which shapes and patterns call out to you?

Sound

(Church bells every hour on the hour marking the hours, days, and seasons; the sound of waves lapping the shore and children laughing at the beach; Miles Davis CDs in the background as you talked on the phone for hours every night at the start of your relationship; the tune from a childhood music box; the crunch of snow underfoot during a midnight walk in a snowfall; the coquis you heard while vacationing in Puerto Rico.)

What are the sounds you envision for your wedding day?

Bride   *Groom*

1. _____

2. _____

3. _____

4. _____

5. _____

Sounds often become an important part of your ceremony and reception, when you know that you want the church bells to ring, or you want to hear your children's school choir, acoustic guitar music during the cocktail hour, pulsing dance music at the after-party. And you want to hear the sound of your beloved's voice in the form of a song he sings to you at the reception, or him proposing a toast to you.

Taste

(Your grandmother's meatballs; a ripe, juicy mango; a butter-soft chateaubriand; tart, refreshing lemon sorbet after a rich, heavy meal; a fine pinot noir served in plastic wine glasses on a romantic picnic in Central Park; strong espresso served in teeny tiny cups; cinnamon gum, a constant flavor on your lover's lips; Mounds bars, freshly baked chocolate chip cookies, still warm from the oven; ice cold lemonade on a hot day; glazed walnuts)

What are some of your favorite tastes?

Tropical fruits? Rich, creamy desserts? (We'll get more into detail on this in the menu chapter of this book, so feel free to be general here—lighter fare, spiciness, textures.)

Bride	*Groom*
1. _____	_____
2. _____	_____
3. _____	_____

4. _____

5. _____

What are the tastes you're thinking about for your wedding?

The dinner she cooked you? A family recipe?

Bride	*Groom*
1.	
2.	
3.	
4.	
5.	

Texture is a very big deal with the sense of taste. Do you prefer creamy or crunchy? Do you *hate* it when things like raisins are embedded in your breads or desserts? Make note of that here. Your caterer will need to know if you're a creamy-crunchy, or if you prefer butter-soft all the way through.

Touch

(Cashmere sweaters; the supple leather of perfectly fitted gloves; the warmth of flannel sheets when your alarm clock goes off on a dark, winter morning; the cool, moist earthiness of terra cotta planters; lush green grass covered in cool morning dew under your feet; bubbles in the bubble bath; the cool tiles of the bathroom floor)

What are your favorite touch-centered memories?

The first time you held hands? The first kiss? The way he places his hand on the small of your back as he guides you into a room?

Bride	*Groom*
1.	
2.	
3.	
4.	
5.	

What are the things you want to touch on your wedding day?

Silk from your gown and gloves? Warm beach sand under your feet?

Smell

(Fresh bread baking in the oven; the lingering scent of your fiancé's cologne on his folded wool sweaters; fabric softener in your Mom's laundry room; the saltwater smell of the ocean; fresh ground coffee during the daily afternoon slump at work; the smell of the air after a rainfall)

What scents bring back your very best memories?

The first meal you shared together? The roses from the first bouquet he gave you? The eucalyptus-scented massage oil she uses on you?

	Bride	Groom
1.	_____	
2.	_____	
3.	_____	
4.	_____	
5.	_____	

Now read these over and circle or highlight the top items that you'd like to involve in your day. Perhaps the speckled blue of the robin's eggs will infuse the color palette, for instance. Telling *your* story throughout your wedding weekend is the whole point of this book.

What do you want your wedding day to smell like?

Lilac? Freshly mown grass? Thanksgiving dinner?

PART TWO

Your Style in Gowns, Tuxedoes, and Rings

CHAPTER 5

Your Dress and Bouquet

A nd now . . . your gown. When you think bridal style, it's
very likely that the first image that pops into your mind is
your gown. Fashion equals style, right? Well, now it's time for you
to further define your style, since you may already have some idea
of what you want to wear on your wedding day. If you're a fash-
ionista, you know the terms and you know the celebrity wedding
dresses you'd like to emulate (Carolyn Bessette-Kennedy, any-
one?). If you're traditional, you might have a silhouette in mind
with wishes to bare your arms instead of covering them with de-
mure lace. You're not at Moment One of your gown definition, so
you don't need the beginner's course. Your goal is to put words to
your style and gown personality.

Let's start off by sending you back to the first four chapters.
Your answers there, in color and fashion sense, undoubtedly
placed the beginning style points for your gown on paper, such as
with your focus on the feel of satin or your fashion preference for
a youthful, sexier look and open necklines, that open back so that
you can feel your sweetie's hand on it while you're dancing.

You've already placed some clues about your wedding gown style. You just have to go back and focus on them. Take a pink highlighter—which you'll use specifically for your gown topic—and circle or highlight any words in those chapters that apply to your gown style. Ethereal, flowing, structured, smooth, regal, natural, pure . . . those words can complete the puzzle. And perhaps not just for you. You might look at a word like *swishy* and see not your gown but your bridesmaids' gowns. Thus, they'll have chiffon-y skirts while you'll wear a column. They'll be swishy while you'll be chic.

To get started, ask yourself the following questions, and answer as honestly as possible:

What's your definition of a bridal gown? What should it convey?

_____

_____

Which aspects of your personality would you like your gown to convey?

_____

_____

What is your feeling about a traditional bridal ball gown? Is it "you," or do you see yourself in something unconventional?

_____

_____

What exactly would make a wedding gown unconventional or daring?

_____

_____

So you have a good idea of your bridal style, but how can you convey that to others? We spoke with celebrity bridal gown designers Michelle Roth and Henry Roth to get their take on how a bride can convey her personal style. Michelle says, "It's hard to believe, but we really do get some 'blank canvases' and have to drag details out of a shy or introverted bride."

"Or, we get a bride who has a long list of what she doesn't want," says Henry. "Which is actually far more helpful than you might expect. Eliminating silhouettes or details helps tremendously in narrowing down a gown style." That works to a degree, but there must be some open-mindedness about your gown style. If you walk into a salon and say, "I am conservative, so I want absolutely no flair whatsoever, no beading, no lace, period!" you could be ripping yourself off. You might be bound in by your limited imagination. You might have formed a rule to live by that has been formed by your everyday wardrobe.

The lesson: Be open to new things.

Yes, you want this to be your style, and you may know that you hate strapless because you dislike your collarbones, but countless brides have been coaxed into a dress on their "no" list that they've absolutely fallen in love with. So in exploring your gown style, promise yourself that you'll at least try on one style you hadn't considered before. You may surprise yourself!

We asked Michelle and Henry to share with us some suggestions for different styles of bridal looks, and here is what they envisioned:

Q: What do you see for a traditional, classic bride?

A: A strapless A-line, like the twenty-first-century princess bride. Brides want to be a modern princess at their traditional, formal weddings, so they may say they want a traditional gown with a modern twist. Or that they just saw Nicole Kidman's formal gown with an asymmetrical one-shoulder top. They don't want the heaviness of Melania Trump's formal gown, or they liked their mother's dress but wouldn't want to wear it. So we'll look at the bodice of that traditional gown, the sleeves, the hem, the train, the fabric, and find out what the bride loves about that gown that she can include in her modern version of it.

Q: What do you see for a garden wedding?

A: Today, you can do a formal dress in satin, a ball gown with a shorter train or princess gown, or you can do an organza strapless dress with a veil, very streamlined and simple to show clearly in a very floral garden. The lack of details in the dress looks more beautiful when there's a lot of detail in the setting.

Q: What about a destination beach wedding?

A: Remember Cindy Crawford's little white slipdress? Everyone seems to want a version of that, or a clean silk crepe or organza dress with a little bit of movement in the skirt. We're seeing low-cut backs and revealed shoulders, halters, strapless, with a veil to the elbow or flowers in their hair. The shape of the dress is simple and chic, or flowing and ethereal.

Q: City-chic?

A: Brides can do lots of different levels with this, from a so-phisticated suit to an A-line, clean, architectural dress. It very much depends on where this city-chic party is being held. Is it in a city loft? That might call for a simpler halter dress with low-voltage embellishments. If it's in a five-star hotel, then the full ball gown with a beaded bodice comes into play.

Gown Formality

Your gown needs to fit the style and formality of your wedding, and that sounds far more official than it actually is. While it's true that traditional rules have changed, and you don't have to wear white, you do have to conform to the rules of formality.

You might not know what your formality level is right now. You might still be dancing with the various images of your wedding day and not yet settled on a location, season, or formality style. So to help you either now or later, here are the general guidelines to wedding day formality rules, and we suggest that you read them not just for informational purposes or "rules," but with an eye toward connecting to the style that feels best to you. You might put a star next to the formality levels you can see for yourself, or you might cross out any formality levels that will defi-nitely not work for your evolving sense of your wedding style. For instance, the casual wedding dress descriptions might make you shudder as an option for your wedding day (but it's a great idea for the rehearsal dinner!). Use these guidelines to help shape your wedding gown style definition, and write your notes here in the book.

Ultraformal (white-tie and black-tie evening celebrations)

- Full-length ball gown _____
- Chapel or cathedral-length train and long veil _____
- Elbow-length gloves as ideal accents to reflect formality

_____

Formal

- Full-length gown _____
- Bi-level gown: long in the back, calf-length in the front

_____

- Chapel or sweep train _____
- In evening, longer train or veil _____

Semiformal

- Floor-length gown is okay! _____
- Cocktail-length gown _____
- Knee-length gown _____
- Fingertip veil _____
- Dressy pantsuit, well accessorized to "dress it up" _____

Informal

- Street-length/knee-length dress _____
- Street-length suit dress _____

* Pantsuit _____
* No veil or train _____

Casual

* Knee-length dress _____
* Sundress _____

Ultra-ultra-casual

* Khaki long skirt and colored or white top _____
* Jeans and floral or solid-color top _____
* Bathing suit and sarong _____

Determining Your Gown Style

Look back at the photos of wedding gowns that you pulled from bridal magazines, and see which style elements initially attracted you. Do you have mostly ball gowns? Strapless dresses? Halters? Your gown style may have emerged by instinct during your first, excited moments of the search. You might know without a doubt that you are "a ball gown woman." If, however, you see a wide range of gown shapes and styles, necklines and bodices, you'll have to explore your true sense of style and define what your dress will say about you. The gown is always an expression of the woman.

True, you won't know that a gown is "the one" until you try it on, but the work you're doing in this section is to give you a focused sense of style—and lots of keywords to describe *you* as well as your dream gown—so that your gown sales associate can offer you the perfect find in a sea of options. Before you get started on the exercises in this section, take a moment and write down the five aspects of your personality that you would like your gown to convey:

1. _____
2. _____
3. _____
4. _____
5. _____

Now, ask your future groom to write down the five aspects of your personality that he most enjoys. Not the five aspects he would want your gown to display, but the five aspects of you, such as your class, your fun-loving nature, and so on.

1. _____
2. _____
3. _____
4. _____
5. _____

Now, you will be able to tell your gown stylist or sales associate the aspects of *you* that you would like your gown to express, which is so much more important than your saying you want your gown to hide your hips or show off your arms. A gown has a personality, and it must match yours.

STYLE NOTES

Part of understanding and expressing your gown style is having the vocabulary that allows you to communicate with your experts, so explore the many, many terms that describe the different types of gown shapes, bodice and neckline styles, train lengths (such as the difference between chapel and cathedral length), even veils and headpieces. You'll find these—*and helpful illustrations* that you can also print out for your shopping excursion—on bridal websites such as www.weddingchannel. com, www.weddingsolutions.com, www.theknot.com, the top bridal magazines' websites, and your favorite bridal gown designers' websites. You'll find starter glossaries at www.sharonnaylor.net and www.botanicalschicago.com, our websites, as well.

Look through the following chart to start matching gown style elements to your personality. Circle the details and keywords that attract you, even if they don't fit in what you *think* your style is. For example, you might like the feather accents from the artistic bride, even though you're a traditional bride. Use this chart to record your own thoughts and descriptions in the margins, and take it with you as you search for your gown. Just the same, take your Possibilities Notebook with you, since you will have written notes on each gown photo you've pulled, just like fashion designers do on their sketches.

Your Style	*Gown Possibilities*
Traditional	• Ball gown with princess neckline
	• Ball gown with sweetheart neckline
	• Ball gown with high neckline
	• Pure white gown
	• Few if any embellishments
	• Pearl or crystal embellishments
	• Long train
Modern Chic	• Column gown
	• Strapless gown
	• Halter gown
	• Pure white or white with color accents
	• Colored pearl beading on bodice
	• Lots of crystals for sparkle
	• Mid-length to short train

Your Style	*Gown Possibilities*
Artistic	• Colored gown in pastels or metallics • Colored gown in brights • Column or A-line gown • Detailed bodice • Visual elements, such as keyhole neckline or illusion netting over the stomach • Feather accents
Natural	• A-line gown or A-line shorter dress • White, ivory, or pastel dress • Floral accents, either in embroidery or fabric accents • Flowing skirt • No train (common style for outdoor wedding)

Your Style	*Gown Possibilities*
Attention-seeker	• Sheath gown • Mermaid gown • Lots of skin showing, such as strapless or high leg slit • Lots of color, such as a bright red gown or bright metallic • Lots of sparkle, such as Swarovski crystals on the bodice, skirt, and train • Dramatic train, such as asymmetrical
Romantic/Historical	• Empire-waist dress • White, ivory, or pastel dress • Flowing skirt • Floral accents • Ribbon or bow accents • Short to mid-length train

Your Style	*Gown Possibilities*

Create your own definition

-
-
-
-
-

Gowns in White . . . or Gowns in Color

Is it your dream to wear the pristine white wedding gown? Does it evoke images of purity, innocence, your childhood vision of "the bride, all dressed in white"? Or are you the fashion-forward bride who thrills at seeing the bridal magazines declaring that wedding gowns in color are *in*. Blush pink gown, baby blue gowns, white gowns with bright red embroidery, sage green gowns with pink satin flowers at the base of a sexy plunging open back, a copper-colored wedding gown with a chocolate sash?

Look through the bridal magazines for images of wedding gowns in color, and tear out all those ads that fit into your vision of the perfect color. Those tear-sheets go right into your Possibilities Notebook.

Whether you're a first-time bride or an encore bride, marrying traditionally or in a destination wedding where you're dreaming of an aqua blue dress to match the ocean, the style in wedding couture is of personalized expression . . . and that means color. Answer the following questions to assess your style preferences and comfort with the trend of color in wedding gowns:

If you are open to a wedding dress with color in it, do you prefer blush hues or bolder hues?

Where would you add color accents to a white gown?

For your after-party, which color do you see yourself in? Bold red? Sparkling silver? A little black dress? What would those colors say about your personal style?

A bride who wears a colored gown is _____ .

CHECK THE TRENDS

www.instyleweddings.com and www.weddingsolutions.com, plus www.theknot.com and virtually every other bridal site and magazine list the top five new trends for each season. If you're the trendy type, be sure to look for the trend style report for the season of your wedding. And even if you're *not* the trendy type, you'll still find modern or traditional inspiration in these lists.

Head to Toe Assessment

You know your best features. You know what you'd like to accent and what you'd like to play down. So your gown style is going to be a combination of *both* these efforts, followed by a deep attraction to a gown's shape, style, and color. It's often the dress you don't think is "your style" that looks amazing on you while it wilted on the hanger, so don't be afraid to take some chances.

Michelle and Henry Roth advise that dress designers and stylists *want* to hear which body parts and features you're not thrilled with. That helps guide them to select gown elements to play up your best features and make you feel beautiful in your gown, whether it's hiding your upper arms, slimming your thighs with just the right skirt, accentuating your waist. We all know that some outfits make us look ten pounds lighter while others make us look wider, and some make our breasts look amazing. So Henry and Michelle say to share those details. "I might look at a bride who hates her arms, but I can't tell that. To me, she looks amazing," says Michelle. "So I want to hear about her arm esteem so that I can respect her feelings."

Michelle and Henry suggest that you write down your feature assessments from head to toe. It's *you* who has to wear the gown and feel amazing in it. So get out a piece of paper and take notes on what you love—and what you dislike—about your body, and then bring this assessment with you when you're gown shopping. Here is your head-to-toe body assessment list, which you can use right here in this book if you'd rather simply star the parts you love or circle the parts you want to play up:

Neck	Upper arms	Thighs
Neckline	Waist	Calves
Shoulders	Hip	Ankles
Back	Butt	Feet and toes
Chest		

Feet and toes? "Yes, a bride will choose open shoes if she loves her feet, or perhaps hide her feet with a more closed style of shoe. That affects the look of the bottom hem of the gown," says Henry.

LENGTHS

The length of your gown will likely be a big style factor for you. Formality dictates a full-length gown for ultraformal and formal weddings, and you may decide that your beach or destination wedding will have you in a knee-length gown that flows with the ocean breeze. So use this space to record your style thoughts about the length of gown that will work best for you.

Are you comfortable in floor-length gowns?

Think back to your experiences as a bridesmaid. Did you like how a column dress made you look taller?

Did you hate the dress that was knee-length in front but floor-length in back, the equivalent of a "dress mullet?"

Your Gown's Fabric

Go back through chapter 4 on the five senses to see what you've written about your favorites in touch. Flip back through your answers in chapter 1 to see if there are memories and outfits recorded there. A satin memory could mean the word *elegance* to you. Cotton eyelet could remind you of your favorite childhood party dress, and you wish to bring the innocence and hope of your childhood to your wedding day. If you went to dancing school and performed in a showcase, perhaps your tutu was made of tulle (and you hated the scratchiness of it!). Or perhaps you remember the butter-soft cotton jersey sheets at a bed-and-breakfast you stayed at together, or the silk dress you wore the night you got engaged, the dress of a stylish older cousin . . .

Think touch-and-feel right now, as well as shine-and-shimmer, and take your perfect keywords from the five senses chapter, any glossary terms you see at bridal sites or at *What's Your Bridal Style*'s article collections at www.sharonnaylor.net and www.botanicalschicago.com, as well as any fabric swatches you've collected, to your gown stylist so that you can feel your way to a gown or dress that suits your style.

ACCENTS AND EMBELLISHMENTS

When you imagine your gown, you might think of a bodice covered with crystal beading, or an appliqué on your train, silk roses at the base of your bare back plunge, even fresh flowers pinned to the same spot. You can add the perfect touch to your dream gown, such as a same-color or blush-colored sash to your waist, or a colored hem to the bottom of your gown for just a hint of blush pink as you walk.

Trains

Matching your gown style to the formality of your wedding to your own preferences, what's your style of train? Does a long, flowing train behind you seem out of date, or the essence of bridal elegance? Do you want a traditional train, or something different from all the others you've seen? Something simple and plain with just a lace edge, or an ornately decorated train with beads and crystals and patterns? A more modern train with color?

When you envision your wedding day look, how do you look from the back or from an overhead view, such as from a camera in a balcony?

Headpieces and Veils

Now you're defining your style for the crowning glory of your wedding look. Your headpiece and veil show off your face, and they're a way to show your personality as well. A traditional headpiece says you're a traditional, classic bride. Something more unexpected like a Juliet cap shows your romantic side, perhaps your love of Shakespeare and the sonnets. A Swarovski-studded veil that catches the light says you're the celebrity of your wedding, with all eyes on you. You shine, so *it* shines. A plain, unadorned veil says you don't need flash to be radiant on your own.

A headpiece can be the perfect accent to your veil, or even worn without a veil depending on your wish for the traditional look versus a modern or natural look without the virginal netting cover. First, though, an important question: How will you wear your hair? Up in a gorgeous updo, or down in loose curls, sleek and straight, or in a chignon?

The answer to that question will play a big part in your headpiece and veil style, since the accents need to work with your hair's arrangement. A chignon might be perfect with a tiara and veil, or a loose, flowing curly hairstyle might be perfect with *no* veil, but rather tiny fresh flowers held in by pins.

Veils

The style of your veil will depend very much on the formality of your wedding, as well as on the design of your dress *and* the location of your wedding. For instance, a formal church wedding might find you in a long, flowing veil, as the essence of the bridal look, while you might want a shorter, puffier veil to dance in the breeze at your beach wedding. The veil is chosen to accent your gown, so your comfort level should make the decision. Do you want a traditional, unadorned veil, or would you like a crystal-edged, light-catching veil to show off the same adornments in your gown? The choice is up to you.

What do you want your veil to say about you?

A bride who doesn't wear a veil is: _____ .

Wedding Bands

Choosing your wedding bands is also an expression of your style. You *don't* have to have matching bands—in fact, few couples go with "the set" these days—so consider your wishes for your band of gold (or platinum!).

Do you want your wedding band to have as much sparkle as your engagement ring, such as a channel-set ring of diamonds, or do you prefer a simpler style without extra diamonds that lets your engagement ring diamond stand out?

What keywords come to mind when you think about your wedding band?

Accessories

The extra touches you add to your wedding day look are as much a statement of your style as your gown. Here, you'll start thinking about the jewelry you'll wear for your ceremony . . . and perhaps a different set for your reception.

What's your jewelry style?

_____ Lots of sparkle! I want to be dripping in diamonds.

_____ Just one piece of flash, like a big diamond necklace, and more subtle earrings.

_____ I want the sparkle on my ears, with no necklace.

_____ I'm more traditional, so I'll wear pearls.

_____ I'm sentimental, so I'll wear my mother's wedding day jewelry.

_____ I'm religious, so I'll wear my cross/Star of David.

_____ I want to wear a spiritual or cultural symbol.

_____ My fiancé is going to surprise me with a gift.

_____ I want color in my jewelry, so it's going to be my birthstone, or red rubies, aqua marines to match the color of the ocean for our destination wedding.

_____ I want the color of my jewelry to have a sentimental factor, such as matching the color of my fiancé's green eyes.

Do you have a family heirloom jewelry set to wear at your wedding? What would it mean to you to wear the same necklace your mother wore at her wedding?

For earrings, talk with your hairstylist—yes, your hairstylist—first to determine how you'll wear your hair, and then choose an earring style that works perfectly for that look. You may find that chandelier earrings look ideal with your chic updo, whereas simple diamond studs work well with your hair worn loose and flowing. Look at your everyday earrings, those hoops and studs and dangles, and decide which styles are your favorite. Most brides stick with what works for them, fearing that a heavier, ornate earring set would feel strange and overpower their look.

When my guests look at me, I want them to notice the following attributes in what order?

_____ My jewelry

_____ My eyes

_____ My smile

_____ My hair

_____ My gown

(This exercise determines the amount of priority you'll put into your jewelry choice. If it's not an element of impact, you can let your eyes do all the sparkling.)

GLOVES

Gloves are most often seen at formal weddings, in a shade to match the wedding gown. Your bridesmaids can wear matching-length gloves in a color to match their gowns, so that you all look extra-elegant and regal.

Answer this: *A woman who wears gloves with a gown looks*

———.

Handbags

Think about this . . . instead of wrapping the jewelry set you'll get for your bridesmaids to wear on your wedding day, why not put the jewelry inside a fabulous, beaded clutch or handbag the girls can use during the day as well. Handbags are the new must-have accessory both for the bride and for the bridesmaids (and also moms and flowergirls). A simple gown style can be elevated in flash level with an eye-catching clutch or oval bag, a Kate Spade bag for your ladies, even bags in theme shapes to match your bridesmaids' own styles. No one says they have to match, so even vintage handbags are open for your consideration.

Shoes

Are you a shoe gal? Do you love your stilettos? Or would you prefer to be barefoot on the beach? Wearing your gown, since your shoe must match the formality of your dress, check out your look in the following shoe styles: ballet slippers, flats, low heels, mid-heels, platform, strappy sandal, sandal with lace or fabric tie, mule, espadrille (for casual or summer looks), and platform. How do your legs look in each? Do higher heels make your calves stand out and your legs look longer and leaner? Are you truly comfortable in higher heels? A thicker, chunkier heel will be more secure for your footing on grass, cobblestone, or gravel surfaces, and perhaps more comfortable through hours of dancing.

Remember, you can wear a higher, more alluring pair of shoes for the ceremony and your photos, then slip into a comfier, appropriate style of ballet slippers for the hours of your reception.

As for color, match your gown, or go for your perfect style of color flash, such as shiny silver heels under that white gown. Your secondary shoes can also have some color, or floral appliqués, even jewel clips attached.

WANT TO DESIGN YOUR OWN SHOE?

You'll love this. At www.stevemadden.com, you can design your own shoe from top to bottom. Every piece of the shoe, from platform to heel to straps, comes in the color and material *you* want.

Your Bouquet

You are the bride. The belle of the ball. The one in the big white dress (or, maybe not after this chapter!). When it comes to the flowers for your bridal bouquet, you can have *whatever* you wish. Your bouquet does not have to match any other element of your wedding. Head to toe, you are the stand-out, one-of-a-kind, focal design element on your wedding day. Nothing about what you're wearing or carrying has to match the cocktail napkins, the ink on the place cards, or the flowers in the centerpieces. As long as the color of your bouquet doesn't completely clash with your bridal party's floral or attire, then composition, size, and flower variety are yours to decide.

You're free to carry something traditional, or something unique, or something completely surprising. If you're having a classic white and ivory wedding in a formal ballroom setting and wish to carry a big bouquet of orange poppies because that is what your groom gave to you on your first date, go for it. If your winter wedding incorporates abundant gatherings of pinecones, seasonal evergreens, burgundy roses, and red orchids throughout, but you have a desire to carry a dainty handful of white lily of the valley because that's what your grandmother carried on her wedding day, do it. If your wedding is a casual, Tommy Bahama–inspired beach theme, but for some inexplicable reason you're fantasizing about a cascading bouquet of white roses, stephanotis, and sweet pea, ask for it. An unexpected bouquet that reveals another layer of your love story, your family history, or your personality is a terrific way to fold your style into your wedding day ensemble, as well as add to your wedding story lore.

Consider the following guidelines when deciding on the design of your bouquet:

- Bouquet composition and size
- Flowers
- Palette

Composition

There are three basic bouquet compositions: clutch bouquets, cascade bouquets, and presentation bouquets. Within each structure, there are wide, wide ranges of style, size and color, and all are open for your consideration as you plan your bouquet style for yourself, as well as for your bridesmaids.

Clutch Bouquets. Clutch bouquets are the most popular bouquet composition for both the bride and the attendants. This type of bouquet is held with both hands in front of the body and naturally hovers near the waistline. Clutch bouquets tend to have a more rounded silhouette and are almost always designed as a hand-tied bouquet: a gathering of flowers shaped into a style, and then simply "hand-tied" together with a ribbon. The stem treatment is very important. Custom cuffs, fabric from dresses, a variety of ribbon banding or braiding, leaf-wrapped stems, buttons, simple bows, and heirloom cameos are great ways to embellish the stems of a clutch bouquet.

Clutch bouquets can fall into many different style categories. This bouquet is incredibly versatile and can be designed to complement just about any dress style and bridal style. Not only is the style versatile, but so is the size. Clutch bouquets range in size from teeny tiny to positively voluminous. Your height, as well as width, allow for larger, more dramatic collections of flowers. Petite brides must be careful not to bury themselves behind bountiful bouquets.

Gorgeous gown details should not be hidden behind a giant

floral arrangement. If your gown is a sleeker, simpler silhouette with few bodice or waist details, you might consider a larger bouquet to accentuate your overall look. You might have chosen a simpler gown because you *knew* your bouquet was going to be the most dramatic part of your ensemble.

Cascade Bouquets. Cascade bouquets are large and flowing, with fresh materials visually tumbling downward. Like the clutch bouquet, this type of bouquet is held with both hands in front of the body and naturally hovers near the waistline, but has the additional size and silhouette of the cascading materials. Cascade bouquets are often designed in white plastic bouquet holders, which are completely serviceable, but real works of art are designed with individually hand-wired blooms and blossoms. Cascades are often pigeon-holed as dated and traditional. But there is a current leaning associating cascade bouquets with very adventurous brides. The designs are trending toward glamorous, over-the-top, and dramatic. The fewer varieties of flowers in a cascade, the more current it looks. When you involve several varieties, the look veers toward traditional.

Cascade bouquets take up a great deal of visual turf. Because of the length, this type of bouquet is best carried by a bride who is taller than average. For more petite brides, the bouquet can just be too much, visually. Also, we find it works best with simple, elegant dresses, or dresses that are quite graphic but with simple lines.

Presentation Bouquets. Most brides conjure up a single image in their mind when they hear the term *presentation bouquet:* Miss America. But please don't let that scare you off from considering this type of bouquet. It is the stiffness and the dull design of that iconic, long-stem red rose bouquet that causes brides to turn up their noses at the thought of exploring this type of composition. Let's look at flexible, graceful, more imaginative flower choices for a presentation bouquet. Presentation bouquets are a natural for the casual bride. The bouquet can be designed quite loosely to reflect a "just picked" essence. For a more formal bride, a presentation-style bouquet might be designed exclusively with a mass of cream-colored calla lilies, or sophisticated ivory French tulips, or vivid sprays of exotic orchids, long graceful stems pulled together with a studied insouciance.

Presentation bouquets are carried in the crook of one arm, forming somewhat of a diagonal across the front of the body. This type of bouquet works better for taller than average brides; not only does the bouquet appear more balanced, but the bride doesn't disappear behind it. This bouquet, like the cascading bouquet, is large and covers a fair amount of real estate along your front, so if your dress is detailed and intricate, don't hide it with flowers.

Flower Variety

How do you determine what flowers you want in your bouquet?

First of all, you need the perfect resource to familiarize yourself with the options. Voilà! The Floral Design Institute website's library, www.floraldesigninstitute.com/page004.06.000.htm, is one of the best online resources for learning more about flower varieties. You have the option of searching by name or image. Since the average person is only familiar with a handful of flower names, the alternative of searching by image will thrill you. Click on the name or image and get instant information. Along with the photo and variety name, there is a verbal description of the flower (you'll sound so smart when describing it!), a pronunciation key for the botanical name (still super smart!), various common names for the variety (just in case, even with the help of the pronunciation key, you still can't pronounce the botanical name), seasonal availability (if you simply *must have* peonies, you'll know to plan your wedding in May or June), the colors it comes in (no, they still haven't developed a blue rose), and then *way* more information than you probably need. But, it makes for fascinating reading if you're the intellectually curious type and want to know everything there is to know about the flowers in your bouquet.

The second step is to answer the following questions:

If you were a flower, what flower would you be? Is it wildflower, a hot house flower, a hybrid? Does the region that this flower thrives in say anything about you? What color? For example, if you picked a rose, expand on that: A creamy garden rose growing in a secret garden in the Pacific Northwest. Super fragrant, very thorny. Does this flower, or any characteristic of this flower, figure into your bridal bouquet?

Are there any flowers that play a role in your love story? If so, jot down what they are and the story behind them. Do you want to include any of these in your bouquet?

Are there any flowers that play a role in your life that you would want to carry close to your heart on your wedding day?

Something from your childhood, like the fragrance from a lilac bush that grew outside of your bedroom window, or the special bouquet of pink roses your daddy would give you (and still does!) on every birthday.

What flowers represent love and romance to you? List the flowers that you dislike and why. Sometimes you'll find a common theme. For example, you might not like carnations and daisies. Why? They're too typical and commonplace. You might not like larkspur, snapdragons, and liatris—too spiky. Sunflowers and gerber daisies—too casual, too bright. Lilies—too fragrant. Calla lilies—too structured and stiff. Make sure you answer the why part of this question. Dislikes are very informative to the design process.

Comb through wedding magazines and websites and actively examine bouquets. Tear out or print out what you love and what you hate. You might have already gathered many images when working on your Possibilities Notebook. Uncover and document the common threads in the images that appeal to you: monochromatic, one to three types of flowers maximum, dahlias appear in seven out of nine of your favorite images, mostly drawn to presentation-style bouquets, and so on. . . . Write down the themes in the bouquets you don't like: too bright, too textural, don't like any of bouquets that have a lot of foliage, the rounded clutch bouquets seem immature somehow.

You've already done a great deal of work with color in chapter 2. When thinking about your bridal bouquet, return to chapter 2 to review some of the resources, such as Sasha Souza's color chart. Also, go back to the list of colors in chapter 2 and note what impressions, words, adjectives, and feelings you wrote down. It is so useful to apply the results of a stream-of-consciousness exercise like that to a specific task, such as selecting the color(s) for your bridal bouquet.

If you have a signature color, what is it and why?

Will that color play a role in your bouquet design?

Do you know what specific color or range of tones you will wear for your lipstick and nail polish?

Will that impact the colors in your bouquet? If so, how?

Something old, something new, something borrowed, something blue. . . . It's just little ol' you, after all, and there are only so many places on your person to fulfill the requirements of this dear old phrase. Will blue be integrated into your bouquet with flowers or, perhaps a simple satin bow? Do you have something old or borrowed, like an heirloom cameo or embroidered handkerchief you would like to incorporate into the design? Are you going to simply skip this tradition because tradition doesn't play into your bridal style?

One final note on color and the bridal bouquet. Strong contrasts of color create a division of visual focus. If you wear white, ivory, or a pale-colored gown and carry a bouquet in vibrant jewel tones or dark, rich saturated colors, all the focus goes to the flowers first. Just for an instant. If you carry a bouquet of colors that blend in more with your dress, thus creating less contrast, focus diverts to your face first. This will be true in person as well as in your photos.

Your bouquet will appear in approximately half of your wedding photos. The first time your groom sees you as his bride, you will most likely have your bouquet in hand. The texture and fragrance of your bouquet will stay with you for a lifetime. Your floral designer, will, of course, assist in drawing conclusions about specifics for your bouquet and the final design. But the thought and energy you have put into the conception will bring it to life.

Bridal Beauty

Of course, the most beautiful gown, headpiece, and veil only serve to show off *your* beauty, so consult with hair and makeup experts to find your perfect wedding day look far in advance of the wedding. Bring your Possibilities Notebook tearsheets of beautiful hairstyles and that perfect makeup application that you saw in *InStyle Weddings*, and work with the professional to determine how best to bring out your personal beauty style. Experts say the best look is a "natural look, only better," so it's up to you to determine how dramatic you'd like to go with your makeup. For your New Year's Eve wedding, maybe you'd like a more smoky eye and redder lips. For your beach wedding, just a bit of bronzer and lip gloss with a touch of waterproof mascara is all the accent needed for your face.

For your hairstyle, is the updo your bridal style? Or does that make your face look too round? If so, a full head of soft curls, perhaps even with extensions to give you a more fairy tale feeling for your day, could be perfection.

Use your Possibilities Notebook to make your notes on your bridal beauty style, any celebrities whose hairstyles you'd like to emulate (such as "Reese Witherspoon at the Oscars!"), or other notes that you can show to your stylists.

Your bridal style has been set! You're going to be gorgeous on your wedding day!

CHAPTER 6

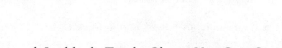

The Groom's Style

Suave. Sophisticated. Laid-back. Trendy. Classic. Very Cary Grant (or George Clooney).

These are the most common words that grooms use to convey their style to a tuxedo or suit specialist when ordering their wedding day wardrobe. While we all know what these words mean, there's a world of variation in what *sophisticated* looks like. And feels like.

Some grooms say they're particularly stumped when it comes to defining their wardrobe style, and many defer to a bride waving a torn-out magazine ad, cooing, "This tux would look *great* on you." When it comes to men's fashion, most need a little bit of help in defining their style on their own. True, some men know their fashion, the lines that look great on them, the fabrics, the patterns, the pinstripes, the lapels, the colors. They've used that knowledge to pick out phenomenal business suits.

However, this is not a business suit for work we're talking about. Your wedding day wardrobe—whether it's a tuxedo, suit, or informal khakis and crisp white button-down shirt for a casual wedding—has a wider range of elements to it than your basic work wardrobe. So, groom, we're starting you off with your intake questionnaire, and your bride gets to chime in with her own answers to specifically-for-her questions immediately afterward. You'll share your answers to move toward your customized definition of your style:

Describe your favorite work suit. What color is it? Fabric?

How do you feel in this suit?

Is it you now, or have you outgrown it?

What five words would you use to describe how you look in that suit?

What five words do you think other people would use to describe how you look in that suit?

If you've ever worn a tux before (and yes, the prom counts), what did you love about the look and feel of it?

Pick out an iconic photo of a man wearing something similar to what you plan on wearing on your wedding day: tuxedo, suit, or casual wear. (For resources, think of classic images such as Humphrey Bogart, The Beatles in Nehru jackets, Ralph Lauren ads). List five adjectives for how he looks in that outfit that you would like to emulate?

1. _____

2. _____

3. _____

4. _____

5. _____

If someone was looking at you from the back, what would they notice with admiration? (Your wide back, your long legs . . . don't be shy.)

From the front?

In your everyday wardrobe, the outfit you'd wear to go out for dinner or to a club, what's the first thing you think about? The color? The fabric? Designer label? How it makes you look? Comfort?

Would you describe yourself as traditional? Trendy? Urban-chic?

Do you incorporate ethnic or cultural elements into your dressing-up wardrobe?

What colors do you look the best in?

What fabrics do you like the best? (This may require a touch-test at the tux rental place or suit store.)

Do you like a matte color or fabric with shine?

Okay, the hard part is over. You expanded your thought process about your ideal look, your ideal impressions, and how you'd like to feel in your wedding day wardrobe.

Now, for the bride's input:

What five words would you use to describe your groom when he's all dressed up—in a suit or tuxedo—for a night on the town?

1. _____

2. _____

3. _____

4. _____

5. _____

What takes your breath away?

What are his best features?

What colors do you like best on him?

If you had to compare him to a male-style icon, who would it be?

Which type of tuxedo or suit would complement your gown or dress best?

Wedding Day Formality

We've started you through your own definition of your groom style. You have some starter words and phrases, perhaps magazine ads or family party photos to convey your wardrobe wishes when you're out shopping. Now it's time for you to blend your style definition into the *definitive* guide to wedding day wardrobe formality rules. After all, an ultraformal wedding demands a white-tie or black-tie tuxedo, no questions asked. Your destination wedding may be formal—with the bride in a traditional wedding gown with train, so what is the groom's matching wardrobe formality rule? We've broken down the categories for your use. Take a look at the tux or suit rules, as well as the coordinating shirt and shoe rules, and then you've further defined your wedding day style when you bring your own personal wishes to that template:

Ultraformal Evening

- Black tailcoat *or* white tailcoat or waistcoat with trousers to match
- Wing-collared white shirt
- White vest for white-tie or black vest for black-tie
- White or black bow tie (tie and vest are in matching color, whether black or white, but the groom is free to wear a white bow tie to set himself apart from his groomsmen and the fathers)
- Black patent leather shoes, or classy white patent leather shoes for the white tuxedo
- Cuff links in gold or silver
- Optional white gloves

Ultraformal Daytime

- Black or gray waistcoat or gray cutaway coat
- Gray pants or gray pinstriped pants or . . .
- Gray cutaway tuxedo
- White wing-collar shirt
- Gray vest
- Gray solid or striped ties or ascot
- Black patent leather shoes or . . . spats
- Gold or silver cuff links
- Gloves (optional)

Formal Evening

- Black tuxedo, tailcoat, stroller coat, or dinner jacket with matching trousers
- White wing-collar tuxedo shirt
- Black bow tie or long tie
- Black cummerbund or vest
- Black patent leather shoes
- Gold, silver, or black cuff links

Or . . .

- Black tuxedo pants
- White or off-white dinner or cutaway jacket
- Black tie, bow or long
- Black patent leather shoes
- Cuff links and other classy accents

Formal Daytime

- Gray cutaway tuxedo or gray jacket with gray pinstriped pants or . . .
- Black or gray morning coat with gray waistcoat and black-and-gray pinstriped pants or . . .
- Light-colored or white jacket
- White spread-collar shirt or white wing-collared shirt
- Ties or vests in color or coordinating print, such as a black-and-gray-striped tie
- Black shoes
- Cuff links and studs

Semiformal Evening

- ❧ Black tuxedo or suit or white dinner jacket with formal black pants
- ❧ White or slightly hued wing-tipped collar or turned-down collar
- ❧ Black or color-coordinated long tie
- ❧ Color-coordinated vest or cummerbund (*Style alert!* Do you want to go formal with a black or white set, or add some color? Keep in mind that a color-matched vest or cummerbund in red or royal blue has a bit of a "prom" look to it, so be sure you're capturing your essence of "wedding" with your choice.)
- ❧ Black shoes

Semiformal Daytime

- ❧ Gray stroller coat, navy or gray suit, or white linen suits in summer or . . .
- ❧ Gray, navy, or black suit
- ❧ White shirt
- ❧ Color-coordinated full-length or four-in-hand tie (optional) or bow tie
- ❧ Gray vest
- ❧ Suit-friendly shoes

Informal Daytime

- ❧ Gray, navy, or tan suit with white shirt or . . .
- ❧ Navy blazer and white shirt with khaki pants or . . .

- White button-down shirt with khaki pants
- Solid or patterned, color-coordinating tie
- Suitable shoes to match outfit

Informal Evening

- Dark suits with white shirts and coordinating ties
- Dark shoes

Ultra-Informal

- Khaki pants or shorts with white or hued button-down shirts
- Bathing suit on the beach
- Suitable shoes or barefoot to match your bride

The Elements of Your Style

A great tuxedo or suit comprises different elements; each an expression of your style.

To familiarize yourself with the different types of tuxedoes, the different types of jackets and lapels, formal evening versus formal daytime rules (i.e., daytime would lend itself more to a gray pinstripe tuxedo) visit www.weddingchannel.com, www.weddingsolutions.com (*great* illustrations of jacket styles!), or www.theknot.com, where you'll find charts and illustrations of different types of jackets. When you're looking at these examples, which thoughts come to mind? ("That's something my father would wear," "That looks very British"). The right style will jump out at you, and of course a tuxedo specialist will further guide you to the right tux or suit for your occasion and your body's shape. Your goal here is to give the specialist an idea of what resonates with you, so that he has something to work with.

Color

While formality rules reign supreme when it comes to picking a tuxedo, declaring that black is right for an evening formal wedding and that gray pinstripe is a fine alternative to black for the daytime formal, and a tan linen suit is fine for an afternoon beach wedding, we're talking now about color. What words, phrases, or images come to mind when you imagine yourself in . . .

Black . . .

Dark gray . . .

Light gray . . .

Light gray with pinstripes . . .

Tan linen suit . . .

A white tux or suit . . .

A cultural outfit . . .

What messages did you get from these images? Perhaps you found that light gray says "wimpy" to you, while the dark gray says "strong" or "classic." The words you've come up with determine how you're going to feel in your tuxedo or suit, so you can eliminate the colors that bring to mind any negative words or memories, and circle the colors that have more positive connotations for you.

Another element that will define your wedding style is the season when your wedding takes place. For summer or tropical weddings, white dinner jackets are a stylish option, as are tan linens. Some grooms request light blue button-down shirts with khaki pants for their informal weddings, or a butter yellow shirt to match the yellow accents in the bride's color-infused gown. In fall or winter, darker colors work best: blacks, navies, and charcoals work now *and* year-round. So follow obvious seasonal color rules.

Now, for the color of your accents: your tie and your vest.

One of the biggest style requests that most men have is that they do *not* want to match their vest and tie to the color of the bridesmaids' dresses. "That's *way* too like the prom," say most. Is that your belief as well? Right now, we see a lot of men choosing to go with an elegant black vest and tie, or a white tie to set the groom apart from the groomsmen. That's the traditional stance.

You, however, might not be traditional. Since weddings are all about expressing personality, some grooms bring their sense of style into their vests and ties. For them, a fun patterned vest and long tie might speak volumes about their fun-loving nature and fashion-forward preferences (e.g., "Hey, Will Smith wore a long tie to the Oscars"), or a burgundy vest imprinted with little sailboats could show your love for the sea . . . and tie in with your marina setting.

It's all about your style. Here are some additional questions to help you explore the more detailed aspects of your wedding style:

If you had to design a tie or vest for your wedding, what would it look like?

What color would you choose? A rich burgundy?

Would it be a solid, or a pattern such as little bottles of wine, or with kitschy Vegas dice on it?

It's your style to create . . . and these tricks aren't only for your wedding day wardrobe—you might think about doing the same for your future business suits or social clothes.

Casual Wedding Day Outfits

We've set this one apart, because a growing number of couples are planning less formal outdoor or garden weddings where a tux would be out of place. For them, the groom might wear khaki pants and a crisp, white button-down shirt, perhaps a navy blazer or a long navy tie. Look at photos of this dress style. You'll see lots of examples in catalogs like J.Crew, where you can get a visual of the khaki and colors look. Once you have some images in front of you, answer the following style-defining questions:

What words come to mind when you look at the pictures? (Preppy, relaxed, etc.)

If you were one of the men at that photo shoot, how would you have felt in that kind of outfit? Like you're wearing a costume? Like you're on vacation? Like the outsider who doesn't belong at the country club?

If you like the image of the relaxed khakis with crisp white or colored shirt, which colors can you see yourself in? Blue to match your eyes? Perhaps a white shirt for you and light blue shirts for your groomsmen?

Use the catalog photo examples to help you, and here's a little secret for capturing the perfect color: go to the catalog website and find the link for that shirt. When it comes up, you'll see all the colors it comes in, and you may be able to click each one to change the color of the image on the screen. This way, you can see what that light green shirt would look like on a model who might even look like you. Then, you simply print it out on a color printer for your shopping trip, or order it right off the site.

MENSWEAR AND BODY SHAPE

Just like the bride knows which type of gown will flatter her figure and make her feel more stylish, comfortable, and confident, so should the groom! There are different options available, allowing you to choose the best suit or tux style according to your body type. You may have already narrowed down your formality and colors, but you've also got to be conscious of how you'll look as a whole in your ensemble. So take a look at the list of bride's body assessment parts on page 59 and note your own. You can find great articles on bridal websites that will help you choose the best tux or suit for your best features. And while you're on those sites, consider the different tie shapes and styles to coordinate your look. Visit www.weddingchannel.com and www.weddingsolutions.com to see the full range of tie silhouettes and lengths.

Wedding Bands

Choosing your wedding band is a matter of style and comfort. You may not be used to trying on jewelry, but you'll know the right one when it's on your hand. (It helps to sneak a glance at the wedding bands worn by your friends and colleagues to get a feel for the detail that you like.)

Do you prefer the simpler style of a plain band with no details whatsoever, or do you want some accent in your ring, such as a thin line of hammered silver? Do you want shine or a more matte look?

What do you think about men's wedding bands with diamonds in them? What does that say about the wearer?

Cuff Links

And now for the smallest detail, which can be a place of great personal expression in your style. What type of cuff links would you like to wear? Consider your self-definition of traditional or trendy, classic or creative, and try on a few different styles at the tux shop. Maybe you consider yourself a traditional man, but you have an aspect of your personality that likes to surprise people. Your classic, traditional tux, then, could show off a surprising cuff link in diamond-chip-centered onyx. You're saying, "I'm traditional, yes, but I like a little indulgence." Here are a few questions to get you thinking about this very important style element:

What kind of cuff links do you own and wear for work?

Do they say "responsible," "sophisticated," "successful?" If you wore them for a job interview, what would you hope they'd say to the interviewer about you?

What do you think about male celebrities' "flash level" with such accessories as diamond cuff links? Do you immediately

*think they're trying to show off, or are you impressed with the
sparkle?*

*If you own your father's or grandfather's cuff links, what elements
of their personalities would be reflected if you wore them for the
wedding? Would wearing their cuff links be a tribute to the lessons
you learned from them?*

Personal Flowers for the Men

First of all, let it be said: You are not *required* to wear a boutonniere. But wearing a boutonniere—a small embellishment of fresh
flowers or greenery—allows you, as the groom, the opportunity for
additional self-expression. So, if you choose to wear one, it will be
the final touch on your clothing ensemble. One other advantage
of a boutonniere is that it will distinguish you from your guests
and your waiters if you have a formal, black-tie wedding.

Black-Tie / Formal

Structured blossoms with distinctive shapes: miniature calla
lilies, spray roses, stephanotis, freesia, and orchid blossoms. The
clean shapes of these flowers stand out nicely against a formal
jacket.

Garden/Casual

Textural items such as herbs and berries: lavender, rosemary, hy-
pericum, tufts of hydrangea, spray roses. A combination of materials works well for this wedding wardrobe style.

Destination

Something local, indigenous, abundant, or traditional to the area: a hibiscus bloom picked right before the ceremony and tucked into a white linen jacket (St. Barthes); an orchid lei (Hawaii); a marigold garland (India)

Seasonal

Take advantage of fresh materials only available during the season of your wedding.

Spring: lily of the valley, muscari, individually wired hyacinth blossoms

Summer: nerine lilies, agapanthus blossoms

Fall: viburnum berries, oak leaves, rosehips

Winter: white pine tips, snowberry, holly

The most popular boutonniere for the groom is to wear a flower that appears in the bridal bouquet. For example, if your bride is carrying a gathering of exquisite ivory miniature calla lilies, you might wear a single ivory miniature calla lily. If she is carrying a gorgeous collection of exotic Mokara orchid sprays in shades of amber, red, and tangerine, a petite trio of amber Mokara orchid blossoms would look smashing on your jacket. A loosely bound bridal bouquet of wild flowers, herbs, and berries might lead you to select a few berries backed with a sprig of rosemary for your boutonniere.

A groom's boutonniere can and should be slightly different from the rest of the wedding party and family boutonnieres. Use this section to check off the spotlight style points that sound good to you:

_____ *Color:* Sometimes the bride and groom carry and wear white and ivory flowers, while the rest of the bridal party carry and wear more colorful flowers, or vice versa.

_____ *Size:* The groom typically wears a slightly larger boutonniere than the groomsmen, ushers, and male family members.

_____ *Complexity:* A boutonniere designed with a few different blossoms as opposed to a single bloom for the rest of the wedding party.

_____ *Detail:* A simple stem treatment such as a ribbon treatment finished with a tailored knot, an Asian-inspired snake grass sleeve to hide the stem, or an organic twist of banyan root.

Your bride will be selecting the flowers for her bouquet; you'll be selecting the flowers for your lapel. There needs to be a visual blend and balance of style: an influx of likes and dislikes, aesthetic influences, history, possibly ancestry, possibly practical issues such as allergies . . .

Tell your story. Who are you as a groom? Record your thoughts in your Possibilities Notebook.

CHAPTER 7

Bridal Party Style

This chapter helps you focus on your style wishes for your bridal party, parents, and kids, and encourages you to work *with* them to select the best wardrobe choices and accents for your wedding day. It can be hard for a group of diverse relatives and friends to agree on any one style, so start this process off by ensuring them their opinions count in the decision. Try and rein in any control freakish tendencies you might have relating to this category. Determine *your* style wishes and then blend in the wishes of others. It is all about the compromise.

Style Notes for Your Maids and Moms

Bridesmaids

Personal style is best defined by the wearer. That's why many brides allow their bridesmaids and mothers to choose their own individual designs of dresses in matching or coordinating colors.

Keep your bridesmaids' personal style preferences in mind

when planning your wedding. Don't require strapless dresses when you know your bustier bridesmaids wouldn't be comfortable with so little support; and don't ask a conservative bridesmaid to dress sexier than she's used to. Find a designer and line that offers customized choices, such as halter tops, strapless, corset, sweetheart neckline or V-necklines, and a choice of A-line skirt or fitted sheath skirt. Your bridesmaids will want to express their individualities, and be comfortable, when they select dresses they actually will wear again.

One trend right now is allowing your bridesmaids to wear different colors. Perhaps your fair-skinned bridesmaids look sallow in light pink dresses, while the other half of your lineup loves how the blush pink looks on them. Grant permission for your fair-skinned blondes and redheads to choose the same dress in a darker hue, one that flatters their appearance and makes them feel wonderful.

A lasting trend has been the little black cocktail dress. When you decree this style as your choice, your bridesmaids may get to wear dresses they already own, or invest in stylish numbers for the future. They will be forever grateful to you for this choice.

Encourage your bridesmaids to use the style definition ideas in chapter 5 as they consider their own best looks, and don't forget that junior bridesmaids should dress age-appropriately. No strapless dresses for eleven-year-olds, no matter how much they want to look like an Olsen twin. Strapless is okay for fifteen years old and up, but the tweens shouldn't be wearing a provocative top—especially if they're just starting to develop (or haven't yet) and are uncomfortable about their appearance.

The key is to have your bridal party's outfits suit the formality of the occasion, using the formality guides in the gown and tuxedo chapters. Cocktail dresses, then, wouldn't be appropriate for an ultraformal wedding, while full-length gowns wouldn't fit for a casual wedding. You must decide the length you want for the gowns and let the bridesmaids know about any restrictions, such as no bare shoulders in your place of worship. The men, too, must suit the style of the wedding—tuxedoes or suits to match the groom's style choice and formality of the day, and they'll wear matching ties to coordinate with one another.

Your bridesmaid dress style definition questionnaire:

Write down the names of each of your bridesmaids, and then write down five words you'd use to describe each of them:

Name	*Description*	
_____	1. _____	4. _____
	2. _____	5. _____
	3. _____	
_____	1. _____	4. _____
	2. _____	5. _____
	3. _____	

Name	*Description*	
_____	1. _____	4. _____
	2. _____	5. _____
	3. _____	

Give your bridesmaids a level of involvement and style definition that other bridesmaids *wish* they had. Ask them to e-mail you the five words they'd use to describe the way they want to look in their gowns, as well as the five styles they hate. Then you have helped to clarify your decision for a matching style dress and you have led them into the same style definition you're using if they'll choose their own gown details.

Mom

Mothers love the freedom to choose their own dresses in their own favorite colors and styles. The mothers may select colors that don't match one another, yet complement their skin tones and favorite colors. For instance, a bridal party wearing light pinks might find the mothers wearing deeper pinks or burgundies. There is no formal rule that the mothers must match or blend with the bridal party. Just try to steer them clear of direct clashing with the bridal party. Don't prescribe a style, but rather accompany your mother and your future mother-in-law on shopping sprees where they too can get the royal treatment in trying on dresses. Provide guidance, but allow the moms to step out in styles that are truly them, or that are a departure they're comfortable with—such as a more modern look for a formerly frumpy mom.

For moms, the general style categories are:

- *Classic*—a formal ball gown with a crystal-beaded bodice and a flowing skirt for a formal wedding, or a classy suit dress for an afternoon wedding.
- *Contemporary*—a stylish, sexy dress when she has the body confidence to wear a strapless top or crystal-beaded bodice with spaghetti straps, and an A-line skirt or long skirt with a slit to the top of the knee. Add in a silky wrap, stiletto shoes, and great trendy jewelry, and Mom looks like a movie star. One mother remarked that she always wanted an occasion to buy Christian Louboutin, and this wedding was it.
- *Conservative*—Mom's more the sophisticated suit dress type, with a cream-colored or blush-colored tailored jacket and full skirt. For afternoon informal weddings or brunch weddings, Mom may even wear a stylish jacket and pantsuit, accessorized with terrific shoes and jewelry.
- *Outdoor*—Mom has her choice of the same formal dress she'd wear inside if it matches the formality and style of the wedding, or a flowing fabric skirt and flattering top in ocean colors or corals to fit in with her surroundings.

To make the most of wedding party style, ask your maids and moms (and maybe even the mothers of any flower girls) the following questions:

What colors suit you best?

Which colors are on your "don't" list?

What neckline are you most comfortable with?

What are your best features and how do you see your dress complementing them?

What are your trouble spots and how can we best avoid them?

What was your favorite formal dress of all time? What did you love about it?

Be open to their individual style descriptions, and ask them to show you examples of their top choices. Remember that budget is often a factor before you select the top finalists for them to consider.

FLOWER GIRLS AND RING BEARERS

Flower girls can wear a white dress, with a color-coordinated sash to match your colors, or a hued dress to coordinate with the bridesmaids. Ring bearers' outfits will match the men, even down to the same tuxedo cut and style. At less formal weddings, the little guys can wear khaki pants or shorts and a button-down shirt to match the men as well. With all children's clothing, be sure you've paid attention to *comfort as well as style.* Get the parents' input on which style of outfit suits the child's disposition, any fabrics that are proven problematic for a child (such as an allergy to synthetics), and age-appropriate style guidance.

Accessories and Shoes

Wedding-day jewelry is often the bride's gift to the bridesmaids, so look back at your descriptions of your bridesmaids for inspiration. The women's jewelry doesn't have to be identical, and the trend is for them not to match. Your conservative sister might love a single silver heart pendant necklace, while your trendier maid might swoon over a modern silver circular choker.

Use this chart to consider your bridesmaids' jewelry styles, thinking about their favorite pieces or the great item purchased during a recent shopping spree.

Name	*Jewelry Style*
_____	_____
_____	_____
_____	_____
_____	_____
_____	_____

When it comes to shoes, it's a whole new world. The days of dyeing shoes to match the dress are pretty much over, as are the days of requiring all of your maids to wear the exact same style of shoe. Now, just ask that they wear strappy silver, gold, or black heels, and leave it to your bridesmaids to select the heel height and width they're most comfortable with.

Flowers

Bridesmaids

For your bridesmaids' and flower girls' bouquet styles, look at the bouquet section on pages 67–75. All of the advice that applies to you applies to them as well. When the dresses don't have to match exactly, neither do the flowers. The key is to keep a consistent size and make sure your choice of color and flower variety is evident, so pick a color palette before you get started.

Moms

Moms are traditionally recognized with some type of flower or flowers, although more and more mothers are opting to forgo flowers in favor of fancy little designer handbags. Also, make sure your mothers realize they do not have to choose the same type of flowers. And, if one mother doesn't want *any flowers,* it is totally fine for the other mother *to carry flowers.* Run through these ideas with them and check off what interests them the most.

_____ *Corsages*—This is the most traditional option, including pin-on, wrist, single bloom, and multi-bloom. Grandmothers usually prefer this popular style, but not necessarily mothers.

_____ *Floral Jewelry*—Intricate and lovely bracelets, necklaces, and chokers can be created with petite blossoms such as orchids, stephanotis, and hyacinth, among others. This style is most often the favorite of today's mothers and stepmothers.

_____ *Nosegays*—Nosegays are typically small, tight bouquets of flowers, miniature versions of hand-tied clutch bouquets. When designing these for moms, go sophisticated and tailored: cymbidium orchid blooms, miniature calla lilies, gardenias, roses. Again, it is fine for each mom to pick her favorite.

_____ *Place Setting Flowers*—If moms don't wish to wear or carry anything, a tiny and unexpected tribute at the dinner table is a nice surprise. When she sits down during the reception, she'll be so happy to discover a petite vase filled with her favorite blooms.

Flower Girls

Flower girls generally carry, toss, and/or wear flowers, depending on their scheduled duties and cuteness requirements. Scan the options below and check off ideas that sound most enticing to you.

_____ *Tossing*—Flower girls can carry grapevine baskets or pails or silk shantung boxes with ribbon handles or anything you can imagine as a receptacle that plays into your ceremony style. She can toss rose petals, hydrangea florets, fall leaves, or orchid blossoms, or any combination of materials that are appropriate.

_____ *Carrying*—If tossing is frowned on or forbidden where you are holding your ceremony, all of the above suggested receptacles look fabulous with an arrangement of flowers inside. Or, she can carry a tiny, sweet, multiflowered nosegay.

_____ *Garlanding*—If you have more than one flower girl of a young age, consider beautiful floral garlands for multiple flower girls to carry down an aisle. This helps provide guidance and keep the little ones together.

_____ *Wearing*—Hair flowers are charming, provided the flower girl is receptive to the idea. If she's not, when the florist approaches her with said flowers, all charm vanishes. Wreaths of flowers are darling. Individually wired flowers to tuck into the girl's hairstyle gives the flower girl and her mother a little bit more control over the look. Hair flowers can be used in conjunction with any of the above options.

For any member of your bridal party, remember: they have the option to express—and change—their personal style. So remain flexible when you first broach the subject with them. The best wedding couples pay as much attention to what their bridal parties feel best in as they do to what *they* feel best in.

It's a matter of finding the perfect fit.

PART THREE

Ceremony Style

CHAPTER 8

Your Ceremony

Without a doubt, your ceremony is *the* most important part of your wedding day. You are vowing to unite your lives and your values, as well as to honor each other in every way possible. Wedding ceremonies are an extremely important part of your day, and that's why bringing each of your styles to the ceremony is philosophically essential to creating a solid foundation on which to build your future.

We'll start you off with some questions to get you focused on this topic. Within your answers, of course, are the keywords and phrases you'll use to express your ceremony style wishes to your officiants and wedding coordinator, as well as notes to *yourselves* for use in the next chapter: how you'll paint your ceremony with elements of your own styles and wishes.

Let's get started with your foundation: what's your ceremony style?

Do you worship regularly? Why?

If you do worship, what or who do you worship?

Do you attend religious services on holidays or family special occasions? Do you do so willingly?

What is your worshipping style? (Some people attend services, while others like to go into a church or synagogue on their own to light a candle and say a prayer; some people meditate, others go for a hike in the mountains.)

Would you describe yourself as spiritual or religious? Define the difference.

Would you describe yourself as agnostic or atheist?

What parts of religion or spirituality do you believe are important in your wedding?

In what way do you think your individual religion or spirituality, or lack thereof, will affect your lives together?

Do you have any desire to become more connected to your faith or a spiritual community? To introduce it to your partner? To explore your partner's faith or spiritual community?

Would your family or your future spouse like you to be more faith-centered? If so, how does that make you feel?

If you're like most couples, these may not have been easy questions to answer. Your faith may have been an unquestioned part of your life, something you embraced but never quite explored enough to put into words. Some couples meet through their faith or their places of worship, but many find each other in different circumstances.

We love to get couples thinking about this portion of the wedding plans, since so many brides and grooms focus on the flowers and the cake, the gown and the tux, the first dance. For some, the ceremony is an afterthought, and while we're not here to adjust your priorities, we are here to get you thinking about your ceremony style. The discovery process, what the two of you learn about each other along the way, is so valuable to your combined future. The way in which the two of you unite your lives *till death do you part* will inform where and if you worship together in the future, how you raise your children, what to expect from each other during holidays and observances, as well as what not to expect. Respect for each other's beliefs is essential. However, you must still ask and answer the hard questions. Get to know each other on this level. If there are irreconcilable differences on the topic of faith, culture, and religion, it is better to be aware of them now and to seek assistance in finding a resolution. This might be a good time to put this book down and let this topic marinate for a while. Think well on the part you'd like your beliefs to play in your wedding ceremony and in your lives, and if you're both of differing beliefs (and have managed to keep that out of your relationship thus far because the rest of your life decisions click just perfectly together), your difference of opinions here is a tremendous gift: it reveals that you have something very important to discuss before you turn this issue into a style issue for your wedding day alone.

It's a common phenomenon that you'll get a tremendous amount of outside influence on your choice of religious or spiritual elements (or lack thereof), and perhaps an argument or ultimatum from well-meaning but misguided parents. The work in this chapter serves an additional purpose: getting you to define your ceremony style so that you can bring it to life unscathed by others' influence. If you can define your wishes, and put your reasoning into words, you'll be prepared should there be a confrontation with your parents or in-laws.

Let's start with a look at the different types of wedding ceremonies:

Types of Ceremonies

Traditional

This style is faith based, and since the rites and rituals come to you from the strict and time-honored values of a house of worship, you will most often receive a "script" of how your ceremony will be run. Traditional ceremonies are culled from the tradition the bride and groom were born into, the tradition of their families, pretty much identical to the wedding ceremonies of parents, grandparents, siblings, and everyone else in the family. And that's just the way some couples would like it to be. They welcome the script, whether untouchable or with allowance to personalize wedding vows, songs, and readings.

Nondenominational

This style of ceremony is spiritual and includes reference to God, but does not adhere to any particular religious protocol. Some couples prefer this style because it can be less restrictive and more open to personalization. It may also reflect the couple's personal style of being religious but not devout or ritual based. A seemingly more "relaxed" version of faith—with all the same depth of meaning—could be the ideal match to your style.

Nonreligious

Nonreligious ceremonies do not refer to faith and typically do not mention God, but rather focus on the promises made between the couple, the fact that the union is now "recognized" and "valid," and may still contain all the romance and meaning of any religious ceremony.

Interfaith

Interfaith weddings feature a blending of two or more faiths, by including aspects of religion or religious rituals or readings that are symbolic of each faith. In many cases, officiants from both faiths are brought together to co-officiate the ceremony, each taking over a portion of the ceremony, each inserting a value or reading or ritual that is important to the bride or the groom. The best of two faiths (or more) can be expertly authored by caring officiants to bring in all the style and belief elements the couple and their families request.

Intercultural

The wedding ceremony, as a joining of your two lives, focuses on the joining of your two cultures, such as a Filipino veil ceremony with a Chinese red string ritual without it being so much about religion. Your officiants or wedding coordinators can guide you on a perfectly choreographed blending of your two cultures, with explanations given to your guests, parents and relatives brought in to participate in cherished cultural rituals.

Spiritual

For those whose higher beliefs don't fit into the neat circles of religious or secular, the highly personalized focus may be on your spiritual beliefs. Some couples gravitate towards beliefs of a universe in control of their destinies, or a New Age or Native American core of belief that recognizes nature. Some call to spirits of departed relatives. Some have specific rituals that are a crucial part of wedding ceremonies. For couples of this mind set, who may have found each other through a spiritual community, it's their deepest truth to have their spiritual belief system reflected in their wedding ceremonies.

Secular

Very much like non-religious ceremonies, this style might be held at home, or at a hotel ballroom, a botanical garden, or any other non-religious site. Again, in a "making this marriage legal" sense, this ceremony is usually led by someone considered "certified" to conduct wedding ceremonies, such as a mayor or judge. Most mayors and judges take this responsibility very seriously, and we applaud those who incorporate inspiring messages into their wedding ceremony scripts. Some infuse humor, and others are known to the family, such as the mayor of the town the bride grew up in who has known her since she was a little girl.

Civil

This is the simple wedding ceremony in the courthouse, led by a judge or justice of the peace, following a "make it legal" script but also open to a warm-hearted judge or justice's wonderful wishes and advice. Some couples do wish to skip the work of planning a wedding, or their life circumstances require that they hurry to the town hall to make their wedding legal. They might plan a more involved ceremony and reception later in time.

Military

Steeped in tradition and military code, these ceremonies often include the service's ranking authority, some content that pays tribute to the lives of those in the service, may be religious or secular, and incorporate rituals that mean so much to the couple who are proud to live the military lifestyle. You might be a third-generation service member or a proud veteran, among our greatest citizens, and your wedding ceremony will reflect this as a sense of who you are, as well as your style and deepest beliefs as a military couple.

STYLE NOTES

An outdoor wedding can be any type of style you desire, from a formal vision with you in a white ball gown with train to a barefoot, relaxed, and casual ceremony on the beach. Catholic ceremonies are not going to be performed in outdoor settings, but you can find wedding officiants to bring in your most desired religious elements to your ceremony. Custom-create your outdoor wedding style and content by talking with your wedding officiant(s) and wedding coordinator.

Chances are, you already know the type of ceremony you're leaning toward. So use this collection of keywords to help you communicate with your officiants and planners. *We'd like our ceremony to be . . .*

traditional	religious	solemn	sacred	holy
devout	pious	uplifting	celebratory	light
humorous	joyful	music based	jubilant	inspiring
secular	spiritual	mystical	divine	colorful
short and sweet	full mass	high mass	family-centric	natural
emotional	not too emotional	inventive	inclusive	unique
simple	intimate	exuberant	festive	

STRAIGHT FROM THE REVEREND'S MOUTH

We asked celebrated wedding officiant Reverend Laurie Sue Brockway, the author of *Wedding Goddess*, to share how she helps her many brides and grooms sort through the swirl of ideas and pressures about their wedding ceremonies to design the perfect ceremony blend that speaks perfectly of their style:

In my line of work as an interfaith and nondenominational wedding officiant, it's all about blending. First we assess the general type of ceremony that is right for each couple. Then we seek ways to blend in the traditions they do like, with creativity, romance and personal touches.

These personal touches can be anything from aspects of

their religions or cultures, to honoring and involving family, to including a humorous story about how they met or a poignant poem that captures their feelings. Or all of the above!

That said, from my perspective, you can create a specially tailored ceremony.

These are some of the questions I ask couples when I consult with them about creating a personalized wedding:

1. Where does religion fit in—or does it?

- Would you like to include an aspect of the faiths you were born into without the dogma?
- Do you want to include mention of God—or would you prefer blessing upon your union without mention of Divine presence?

2. What kind of ceremony would be most suited to the two of you?

- Would you like something personal yet that includes *aspects* of your traditions?
- Or would something romantic and offbeat be more your style?
- On the spectrum between a formal and traditional ceremony and the wackiest exchange of vows you can think of, where are you? Somewhere in the middle or somewhere on the edge, wanting to be different?

3. What are your special needs?

- Think about the requirements you each may have. Is one of you more religious than the other?
- Is one of you atheist or agnostic?
- Are you an interfaith pair?

- Do you hail from different cultures?
- How much do you want to honor your heritage and the traditions of your parents and family, etc.?
- Is there anything you abhor about those traditions and would never want in your own ceremony?

4. **What do you two truly want? Most important, be completely honest with one another (and then, your officiant). Make sure you are creating this ceremony for the two of you—not just to please others.**

I give couples this mantra to adhere to as they seek to create a ceremony all their own: "We will create our wedding ceremony our way."

Rev. Laurie Sue Brockway is an interfaith and nondenominational wedding officiant, and the author of *Wedding Goddess: A Divine Guide to Transforming Wedding Stress into Wedding Bliss*, www.WeddingGoddess.com.

Be honest with each other, with *yourselves*, and then with your officiants. In no other area of the wedding plans is truth more important, because your wedding ceremony is based on truth. So if you're not able to decide on your wedding ceremony style at this moment, do *not* rush to a decision just to make someone else happy. You never have to make a final decision on anything in this book after just one glance at a chapter, and that advice applies exponentially to your wedding ceremony. So take your time, work through the questions at the start of this chapter, take time

to talk with each other. Talk to your officiant or to a separate religious leader or counselor if you're reaching an impasse between
yourselves, and work on this all-important issue—not just for the
wedding but for the future. You can't have your wedding reflect
your faith and beliefs if you don't know what they are, or if you
can't communicate them with each other.

CHAPTER 9

Ceremony Elements

You've defined the type of ceremony you want—or are at least on your way to a true definition—and now it's time to fine-tune your style of ceremony elements: your vows, music, readings, special tributes and rituals, and of course, the look of your ceremony.

If you're planning a traditional, religious ceremony in a house of worship, be prepared for "the rules of the house" before you invest any time in defining your ceremony style. The elements of your ceremony will be more scripted. You may get a list of approved readings, approved music, approved décor, and other rules that many houses of faith prescribe in their efforts to keep up their time-honored rituals. This is not to say that you have absolutely no choices or style incorporation at these institutions—in fact, many denominations or individual officiants in even the strictest houses of worship do allow a degree of personalization. You may, for instance, be allowed to request changes or additions to the traditional wedding vow script—removing *"obey,"* for instance. But secular music might still not be allowed at all.

Work through this chapter together, as your ceremony is the most important part of your day, and return here several times if inspiration arises throughout your planning process.

Readings

Readings add an extra dimension of meaning to your ceremony, perhaps expressing your thoughts about love and marriage through the use of ancient, classic, or modern writings. Not all couples want the lengthy, albeit inspirational, recitation of religious or secular passages shared as part of their rites, so think about what level of depth any reading will bring to your ceremony . . . such as poetry or psalms that describe you as a couple. Since these questions will inspire detailed answers, use your Possibilities Notebook to record your thoughts together and individually.

What do you think about the "traditional" ceremony readings that might be pertinent to your faith, as performed by family members and friends, the officiant, clergy, your children, your parents, etc.?

Describe your favorite poems or song lyrics.

What are your favorite verses of religious writing, such as from the Bible, the Koran, the Torah, or other holy books?

Do you have a favorite author and/or poet whose work speaks perfectly to your union? If not a particular writer who you can identify, a favorite quote, passages, chapter, sonnet, poem, or well-known plaque quote.

What readings have you found moving at wedding ceremonies you've attended? If so, what was conveyed and why did it strike you?

Music

Music brings a range of feeling to a wedding ceremony, such as the awe of traditional wedding music ("Wedding March" or "Ave Maria") or the light and contemporary mood you want, such as an upbeat song played during your recessional that says, "The ritual is done, now it's time to celebrate." You may choose the songs from your love story, or a song that describes your partnership perfectly. Again, use your Possibilities Notebook for your descriptions and lists.

Which types of music move you and convey the feeling and ambience of the wedding you envision? Classical music? Reverent organ music? Upbeat piano music? How does that music make you feel?

Now imagine a ceremony that is devoid of all music—what would that feel like to you?

What are your favorite traditional wedding songs? "Wedding March"? "Jesu, Joy of Man's Desiring"? "Trumpet Voluntary"? "The Four Seasons" by Vivaldi? (Listen to a wedding music CD from the library, or listen to songs online, to get a good feel for the time-honored bridal music classics, and ask your religious officiants for CDs of traditional songs in your particular faiths.)

What are your all-time favorite love songs?

Which songs have you deemed "Our Songs" throughout the history of your relationship? (You'll not only use one of these for your first dance at the reception; one or more can be used within your ceremony.)

Do you prefer instrumental music for your ceremony, or music with lyrics?

Do you prefer an original recording—which can be played through a sound system at most sites—or do you want live musicians, a choir, a pianist?

Which instrument(s) would you like playing live at your ceremony?

How many songs would you like played during your ceremony, and at which points in the ceremony? Think about arrival time, music playing as you light the unity candle, family tributes, etc.

Which song would you like to play as you walk down the aisle? Something traditional? Classical? Contemporary? Sentimental? Unexpected?

Do you have a friend who can perform music or an original song during your ceremony? (If not during your ceremony, this could be a wonderful style point for your reception.)

What do you want the music to convey during your ceremony? Joy? Praise? Romance? A sense of place, such as music to match your garden wedding or island wedding?

Vows

Your vows are your everlasting promise. What exactly are you promising? Examine a set of traditional vows and see if it speaks to your relationship. It may be your personal bridal style to "stick to the script," or to say the same vows your parents took, which would give your union a deep level of meaning and family sentimentality, or you might wish to infuse humor or include anecdotes from your love story.

Use your Possibilities Notebook to give you plenty of room to record your thoughts.

Do you wish to follow a traditional wedding vow script, or do you wish to personalize your vows?

If you'll personalize your vows to any degree, even just changing a phrase within the traditional script, adding fresh expressions after the traditional script, or writing all-new, custom vows, do you want to write one version that you'll both repeat to each other, or do you both want to write your own original vows?

Are there any quotes or poetry lines that are perfect for your vows?

Do you want to share your original vows with one another before the wedding, or have them be a surprise gift to each other in the moment?

What are the things you love about your partner that you wish to convey in your wedding vows?

What are the things you wish to promise one another in your wedding vows?

Will you use humor in your wedding vows, as a way to sound like yourself? Or do you consider it a mark of respect to use formal wording?

What would you like your partner to promise you?

If one or both of you have children, will you take vows with your children as well as with each other?

Name some of the qualities of original wedding vows you've heard at the weddings of friends and relatives that have resonated with you.

Think about wedding scenes in movies, on television shows, and on celebrity wedding specials. Does anything stand out as a "must" for you? If not the wording, then the style?

Religious, Spiritual, and Cultural Elements

Do religious, spiritual, and cultural elements carry much weight in each of your lives, or in your lives as a couple? How big of a part? Do each of you come to the relationship with differing influences in these areas? One of you might prefer a purely religious ceremony, while the other might want more spiritual elements such as hand-fasting. It can take a little creative work for you both to custom-blend your styles in a unified ceremony that reflects *both* of your belief systems. Use the guidelines below to fine-tune your ceremony's deeper meanings and symbolic rituals:

Before you start listing religious, spiritual, or cultural elements, write down the five adjectives that you'd like your rituals to convey ("unity," "romance," "protection," "abundance").

Are you considering adding any rituals to your wedding to make others happy? If you're getting pressure to include a ritual, write down how you feel about the ritual in question.

What would you like each of your ritual(s) to bring into your ceremony?

Ritual	*Meaning*

❧

❧

❧

STYLE NOTES

Enjoy the learning process of finding out more about the wedding rituals of your partner's faith, spiritual beliefs, or cultural heritage. You might find as you search online or talk to family elders that the rituals you thought you understood have even deeper meaning to the family. As you look, listen, and learn, some rituals could become a "must" for your ceremony style *and* become a part of your future family celebrations.

Would you like to "twist" a traditional ritual, such as doing a unity sand glass instead of a unity candle. (This tradition is brand new. Instead of lighting a unity candle—which may not work on a breezy beach—the couple pours snifters of natural- or pastel-colored sand into an attractive vase to keep forever.)

In an interfaith ceremony, which elements of your faith's ceremony are most important to you? Which are non-negotiable? (Be prepared to explain this to your officiant(s), as they're most invested in creating the ceremony of your dreams. They will definitely want to know what you'd like them to read, to sing, to offer.)

Tributes

Ceremonies are quite emotional and certainly bring to light those important figures in your life who are not able to be there to share it with you. We all like to think those people are with us in spirit, and we're sure they are. Use your Possibilities Notebook to record your wishes.

Who would you like to walk you down the aisle?

How would you like to honor your parents at the outset of the ceremony, or within it? Perhaps you'd like the officiant to address your parents directly, thanking them for the tremendous job they did in raising you? Or would a simple kiss on their cheeks before they walk you down the aisle say it all?

How would you like to honor a departed parent? With a reading of his or her favorite quote? The officiant's opening remarks about how your parent is with you in spirit? A brief address by a relative or family friend, saying how proud the parent would be?

How would you like to honor other departed relatives and friends? With floral arrangements? A lit candle? A rose on an empty chair?

How can you pay tribute to your children? Taking vows with them? Giving them a gift after you exchange rings?

The Décor

We've talked a lot about faith, culture, music, and of course, vows. Now let's examine what your ceremony *looks* like. In this section, we will list some of the basic elements you will want to *consider* addressing in terms of your décor as well as a list of opportunities for décor possibilities. When you're having your ceremony in a house of worship, generally speaking, you need fewer décor elements. When you're having your wedding ceremony in a nonreligious environment, you often need more elements to define the space.

Consult the chart below. First, where is your ceremony being held? Look to that column for some of the *basic elements* to consider, then review the list of *opportunities* for décor. Highlight the items of interest to you and your loved one.

Church	*Synagogue*	*Secular Venue* (hotel, hall, tent, museum, club, inn)	*The Great Outdoors*
BASIC ELEMENTS			
aisle runner	chuppah	aisle runner	a rain plan
pew décor	aisle runner	aisle décor	a good view/backdrop
focal pieces	chair/pew décor	focal pieces	aisle décor/definition
	focal pieces	stage and stage covering	focal pieces
		rented step for stage	

Church	*Synagogue*	*Secular Venue* (hotel, hall, tent, museum, club, inn)	*The Great Outdoors*

OPPORTUNITIES

Architectural Embellishments	**Architectural Embellishments**	**Ceremonial Structure**	**Ceremonial Structure**
balcony railings, existing urns, outdoor planters, front doors, ledges and alcoves	balcony railings, existing urns, outdoor planters, front doors, ledges and alcoves	arch, chuppah, mundap, canopy backdrop	existing pergola or arch, chuppah mundap, canopy tree décor landscaped aisle
unity candle	candles or candelabra	**Architectural Embellishments**	**Architectural Embellishments**
Virgin Mary flowers	lighting	balcony railings, existing urns, outdoor planters, front doors, ledges and alcoves, fountain	balcony railings, existing urns, outdoor planters, front doors, ledges and alcoves, fountain
sign of peace flowers			
candles or candelabra		lighting	existing garden beds or lawn
arch or arches			existing pond or pool
lighting			lighting

Now that you have a handle on what areas or elements of your ceremony you would like to focus on with décor in mind, let's take the next few steps that explore the personality, priorities, and palette for your ceremony.

Personality

Your ceremony is an event in and of itself, with its own personality and rhythm that is distinctly different from the cocktail hour, the reception, and the after-party. Use your Possibilities Notebook to go in-depth with your ideas and answers.

What is the personality of your ceremony? You'll be relieved to know you've already done the work to answer this question. Just take a moment to gather all of the answers in one place.

- What type of ceremony are you leaning toward: Jot it down here. Return to pages 108–111 to see the types of ceremonies.
- Return to page 112 to see what key adjectives to describe the mood of your ceremony appealed to you. Jot them down here. If you didn't find ones that inspired you, write in your own.
- Return to chapter 1 to see what style categories intrigued the two of you. Jot those categories down here, or write your own.

These are the words, adjectives, and styles that shape the personality of your ceremony. Consider the information you've gathered throughout this chapter: location, design elements, type of ceremony, list of adjectives to describe the feeling you want during your ceremony, and your style categories. This collection of information is a wonderful springboard for the imagination. It will inspire your choices; it will inspire your design team.

Priorities

Most engaged couples are working with a budget, so prioritizing your wants and needs is essential. Meet with a designer and share what you know about the location, type of ceremony you're having, design elements you wish to explore, and the personality of your ceremony. Work with them to flesh out the design ideas. The creative process can and should be a stimulating volley of ideas between you and your designer. Then, request a proposal with a list of itemized pricing for the designs. Sync up the design ideas with the available dollars. If your budget is not large enough to cover the cost of the design, figure out what the most important elements are practically *and* emotionally. The act of prioritizing has an enormous influence on the décor. It will determine whether something is lavish or simple, over-the-top or understated. But, even in simplicity, even with just a few elements, a great deal of your style will shine through. It might be a perfect expression of your priorities to downplay any décor and have the two of you be the main attraction.

Palette

Your ceremony décor doesn't have to match the color of your bridesmaids' dresses or the colors of your reception. The ceremony has its own personality, so it may have its own color palette as well. Return to chapter 2 to review your emotional responses to color. Blend these responses, plus the information you've gathered about wardrobe, type of ceremony, and personality ceremony, to see how those choices influence your palette. Jot down some initial colors or color combinations here.

1. _____

2. _____

3. _____

Putting It All Together

Here is an example of how personality, priorities, and palette worked together to help a bride and groom determine their ceremony site style. You'll see that they are the foundation of style definition, with the couple free to add their own personal touches. The elements the couple has chosen to focus on are in italics.

Outdoor Wedding Ceremony/Nondenominational/ Style: Asian

Personality: *Serious, beautiful, bearing emotional gravity, peaceful, deep*

Palette: *Shades of pink, chocolate, and apple green*

Set among a gorgeous arbor of cherry trees in full bloom at a botanic garden or on a private residence or rental property. (See www.nybg.org for a look at the New York Botanical Garden as inspiration.) Mother Nature designs the most focal feature of your ceremony. The soft, pink petals of the cherry blossoms alight on the dark wooden branches of the tree create a breathtaking environment for your union. Dark wood bamboo chairs spiral around a low stage, creating the setting for a *ceremony in-the-round*. The wooden risers that compose the *stage* are tastefully and precisely box-pleated with a heavy, apple-green muslin fabric.

A simple, yet dramatic square of apple-green silk dupioni edged with a wide border of silk kimono ribbon in varying shades of pink is delicately suspended from overhead tree branches, creating a soft, slightly free-form *canopy* over the stage, further defining the focal point of this event. The *chairs* lining the central aisle along which the bride will travel are adorned with bundles of cut, blooming cherry branches, loosely gathered and tied with sheer, wide apple-green ribbon. The bases of the branches touch the ground and the tips of the branches reach a good two feet above the back of the chair. The ribbon is loosely knotted and the sheer streamers stir lightly in the spring breeze.

The start of the central *aisle* is flanked by a pair of electric, freestanding "water fall" fountains, which will set the tone for your ceremony with their peaceful babbling. Since the ceremony will occur during the late afternoon, *lighting* is not a key concern, again, Mother Nature will take care of that for you. But to soften and continue to define the area, several apple-green paper lanterns in varying sizes are hung from tree branches over the circular seating areas.

The *rain plan* will be to hold the ceremony in a tent, sans cherry trees. The fabric will be canopy and lanterns will be suspended from the tent's crossbars, and the rest of the décor elements will be utilized as planned.

Priorities: Cherry trees, in bloom. Find a *venue* that has an abundance of cherry trees, such as a botanic garden, a rental venue with a garden, or a private residence. Cherry trees in bloom are the key priority, so the *season* for the ceremony must be thoroughly investigated. If that doesn't come to fruition, the cherry blossom branches attached to chairs and additional elements will help to make up for the coveted cherry trees . . . but, there still need to be trees. Additional priorities include Asian influence revealed throughout the design, creating focus for the ceremony itself, as well as the journey down the aisle of the bride to the groom. Balance.

Invest time in considering the place where you want to be standing when you take your wedding vows. You get to be the creator. You get to decide what will surround you, as well as whom. Enjoy this process of playing "set designer" for your ceremony, as well as "author" of your wedding ceremony as a whole. You'll get to do this again with regard to your reception.

PART FOUR

Your Reception

CHAPTER 10

Reception Style

Not all wedding receptions are of the traditional "cocktail party followed by five course sit down dinner" variety. With so much personalization in weddings, and with more couples vowing to do something *very* different from their friends' and families' weddings, you have many opportunities to express your style. Before you take any steps in this chapter, look back at what you wrote down for the "personality" of your reception, and use that as one of your keywords while planning. Your top initial style definitions will open up as you move through the process, so consider them map markers to guide you to your original, unique, and personally styled reception.

Originality is key, and that will come from your keywords. "Everyone has had that usual dinner reception," says one couple from New York City. "We've been to a dozen weddings this year, and they're all too much the same. The salad comes out, the entrée comes out, blah blah blah. That, to us, is a cookie cutter wedding, and we wanted something entirely different. So we arranged for seven different stations plus passed hors d'oeuvres, and the guests helped themselves from those throughout our entire five-hour reception. Everyone *loved* it."

While we'll get into the amazing and unique food choices that might fit your most authentic and personalized reception style in chapter 11, let's first figure out your style of reception *type*. Check off those that appeal to you right now, without any thought about budget. Money doesn't dictate style, since any type of reception can be planned on a budget. So don't let financial anxiety warn you off of a style that's "you."

_____ *Traditional cocktail party first, then a sit-down dinner.* The cocktail party is most often a mix of buffet, stations, and passed hors d'oeuvres, and the sit-down dinner is anywhere from three to seven courses, depending on your choices.

_____ *Two-level cocktail party reception.* If you love the mingling aspect of a cocktail party, rather than the more formal sit-down at your assigned tables to eat during the dining hour of the reception, you're more gregarious and less structured, more social, more informal. You love the flow of a cocktail party, and you love offering unique foods at the food stations and buffets, with additional hot or cold hors d'oeuvres passed by servers. The two-level category means that you have a first cocktail party, maybe a traditional form, and then everyone moves into another room for a themed cocktail party—such as a Moroccan theme or a Tuscany theme. Guests love this new trend for its uniqueness and the cultural tastes on the menu, even themed drink and live entertainment.

_____ *Traveling reception.* In keeping with the mixing and mingling, "go to a new room" style, this reception takes your entire group to three or four different locations, each with its own theme. So you might start in a traditional cocktail party room, then move outside to a terrace, then go into a ballroom for dinner, then walk out to the pool area (which is now lit with blue lights and tiki torches, with lights in the trees) for the dessert hour. The eclectic couple loves this style, the always-on-the-go couple who didn't want to choose between their four favorite styles. They found a way to use them all!

_____ *Buffet reception with passed hors d'oeuvres.* You'll stay in one place, and the entire reception is an extended four- to five-hour buffet in a vast array of food choices, with stations, and hot and cold hors d'oeuvres are hand-passed by waiters. It's a fallacy that this type of reception is less expensive than the traditional cocktail hour and dinner model, as prices are still figured per head and according to the menu items you choose.

_____ *Buffet reception only.* You've stocked your buffet with tasty hot and cold menu items, and the buffet tables may be spread around the room. You might have servers there to help guests, or it may be a do-it-yourself style. This reception is less formal, and you might incorporate some stations as well.

_____ *Stations with passed hors d'oeuvres.* Couples love their food stations. So this style of reception is set up formally, not like a street fair or carnival with food stop after food stop. For this style, the stations may remain the same throughout the night, or you might switch in a few new styles for the second half of the reception.

_____ *Dessert and champagne*. Forget the shrimp cocktail and the lemon chicken. This nighttime reception is all about the desserts, served with fine champagne, wines, and liqueurs. From cakes to mousses to chocolate-covered strawberries, tortes and fruit pastries, bananas foster or a chocolate fountain, the menu is sweets. And plenty of them. Couples who don't want to emulate others' weddings, and who love their desserts, often choose this style of reception for its novelty, indulgence, and friendly budget amount.

Some questions to help discern your reception style:

Do you want your guests to spend large blocks of time seated at their tables, or do you prefer mingling? _____

Will moving to new locations be practical for some of your elderly or disabled guests? _____

Does your wedding site lend itself to a multi-stop reception?

_____

If you'll have a second themed cocktail party as your reception package, what would the theme be? _____

Are you trying to decide between several different menu themes?

_____

Which elements of your reception would you like to keep traditional, and which would you like to be creative with?

You'll soon move into the menu chapter, where you'll work more on your food choices and themes. If you're not clear yet on your reception style, it's very likely that your penchant for stations or your cultural food choices might make this decision for you. But put your appetite on hold for just a little longer while you consider the next most important element of your reception—the décor. The best food in the world will be even better when you design a reception setting style that's perfection.

Defining Your Reception Style

The reception is home to many important wedding events. It's where you will be announced for the first time as a married couple, where you'll share your first dance, where you'll cut the cake. It's also where you'll connect with all of the people who have come from near and far to cheer you on as you begin this new phase of your life. All of your style choices, from the save the date cards you picked way back when, to your floral centerpieces to the favors, culminate in this event. It is the main course of your wedding day. Use your style wisely and you will make an indelible impression on your guests by throwing a one-of-a-kind reception.

When thinking about your reception style, it comes back to the simple parameters once again of personality, priorities, and palette. Discuss the following factors, and they will lead you to a spirited conversation that kicks off the design process for your wedding reception.

Personality

Several factors play into your reception's personality: the venue, the time of day, and the meal you will choose to serve.

There are very few venues that are perfectly neutral. Venues are often selected because the existing style is agreeable to the bride and groom and plays directly into their reception style or because the venue is quite malleable and can be *transformed* into their reception style. Sometimes, outside influences such as parental influence, club affiliations, dates, or budget force you to select a venue that might not be your *dream* venue. Regardless of how and why you decide on your venue, it will have an impact on the style of your reception. Incorporate it or transform it, but don't ignore it.

The time of day and the food you'll be serving will define your reception as a breakfast, brunch, luncheon, cocktail, buffet, or sit-down dinner wedding. Many styles and levels of formality can be relayed through each of these meals. You can certainly have a city-chic brunch or a casual sit-down dinner. But, the pace and the flow of a reception revolve around what you serve and how you serve it.

Use your Possibilities Notebook to record your ideas and wishes, and share these notes with your experts.

What does the style of your venue communicate to you?

Does your venue set the tone for your wedding? If yes, how so? If not, why not?

Describe the style elements of your venue that you wish to highlight.

Describe any style elements of your venue you wish to minimize or cover up.

What time of day are you choosing for your wedding reception?

What meal is your reception going to revolve around?

How does the time of day and the meal you've selected for your reception play into the level of formality you would like to establish?

Before diving in headfirst to your conceptualizing your reception design, realize how many inspirations you've already generated throughout the first half of this book directly apply to your reception style. Draw inspiration from those initial reactions and insights for your reception. Being prepared with answers to the above questions, presenting images from your Possibilities Notebook, as well as possessing a few key adjectives that embody the personality you'd like to establish for your reception will set you on the path to a fully realized design.

Priorities

Prioritizing your style elements in accordance with your budget is a difficult assignment. It isn't every day that you buy flowers, rent linens and lighting, and fund custom-made backdrops. You need to have an idea of what things cost, as well as what you can afford to spend. If you're working with an event planner, they can certainly help to guide you in this area, as can people you know who have recently been married. The latter can be especially helpful if you've attended their wedding and seen what that budget accomplished for their reception. When you call to make appointments with florists or event designers, ask if these vendors have a minimum. Ask what their average wedding runs. If you don't have a specific budget in mind, at least have a range. Giving realistic parameters to the designers you meet with is important. It will help them guide you in the right direction for your design *and* your budget. The last thing you want is to be presented with a décor budget that embodies everything you want visually, but is so far out of reach in terms of what you can spend, that it is unattainable. It is impossible for a designer to present a couple with solid, unwavering numbers prior to sitting down, understanding your needs in terms of style, and fleshing out a design.

When faced with the choice of where to pare back, if need be, let your designer work with you on this.

Palette

Consider how prominent the venue's color scheme is, or is not, and what bearing it will have on determining your color palette. Consider the season, as well.

Are you going to work with your venue's established palette, if there is one, or against it? How?

Will the season affect any decisions you make regarding palette? How?

Use your chapter 2 responses to color. Blend these responses, plus the impact of the venue and the season (if any) to see what you come up with regarding a palette for your reception. Try out several different ideas, just for the heck of it. Sometimes seemingly outlandish possibilities lead to a truly inspired palette.

Welcome input from your on-site contact, as well as your designer. Typically, they know the space incredibly well and have had the opportunity to see a multitude of palettes. They'll have some valuable suggestions on what works and what doesn't.

Style Components

Here's where you literally become the artist of your wedding day. To help you decide on your style *components* of your reception space—those must-have elements like the cake table and a photo display table, floral décor, and more—take a piece of 8 x 10 paper and outline the shape of the reception hall room. It might not be a true rectangle, but may have nooks or an L-shape to it. Then, use it to sketch in all the components you want for that space. For instance, you'll mark where you want your cake table, and so on. To determine your code, consider the following arrangement (or create your own!), using it as a checklist to make sure you include essential elements:

Black marker indicates the placement of furniture

_____ Cake table

_____ Dance floor

_____ Gift table

_____ Guest tables (the site staff, caterer, or event designer can
help you with sizing and spacing)

_____ Head table or sweetheart table

_____ Lounge area

_____ Piano

_____ Place card table

_____ Stage for band/location for DJ

Green marker indicates the placement of florals

_____ Accents for the cake table

_____ Centerpieces

_____ Focal floral or decor throughout the room

_____ Garlands

_____ Outside urns and planters

_____ Windowsill and mantel pieces

*Blue marker indicates the placement of food stations and
drink stations*

_____ Bar

_____ Dessert stations

_____ Food station

Yellow marker indicates lighting wishes

_____ Candelabra/candle placement

_____ Chandeliers/sconces

_____ Lighting on dance floor

_____ Pin spot on cake table

_____ Pin spots on existing artwork

_____ Pin spots on guest tables

_____ Pin spot on the head table

_____ Uplighting or ambient lighting

You can make up your own additional categories and codes to indicate the style choices you are envisioning for the room. Use this system as you assess reception sites, or wait until you decide on and book your final choice. But it does give you the map that will allow you to define your style components to share with your site manager, floral designer, caterer, and others.

For an outdoor wedding, you'll create the same map, noting where you would like landscape lighting, entrance pathways, dance floor or tent, and so on.

STYLE NOTE

Look up! You don't just get to work with the shape of a floor plan, filling it with tables and buffets. Your style can be displayed in the *air*, such as floral pieces hanging from tree branches, colorful paper lanterns strung between trees, strings of lights around the outline of your tent, strands of orchids hanging from chandeliers, strings of crystals or flowers descending from the ceiling or tent or trees. Use the entire space of your reception site to express your bridal style.

Flowers

Wedding receptions rarely happen without flowers. No matter the size or style of the reception, each table will beg for the attention of some type of centerpiece. Not to mention the entrance, the place card table, and the ladies room. Don't limit yourself to traditional blooms: fruit, plants, candlelight, exotic wood, and sculpture are a few elements to consider when imagining design possibilities.

Below is an exploration of a few style categories and some possibilities for the floral design, just to get your imaginative juices flowing. These are simply ideas, nothing definitive. This exercise illustrates how style categories transform into design.

Style Exploration: Flowers

Classic. Gorgeous arrays of flowers in shades of white, ivory, and champagne, accented with touches of chartreuse, designed in elegant, silver-plated vessels. Featured flowers might include fragrant lilies, open roses and spray roses, arching Hawaiian dendrobium orchid sprays, bells of Ireland, and calla lilies.

Zen. Collections of large, geometric glass vases in varying sizes filled with water and topped with floating candles. Submerged under water within each vase slender grasses, bamboo, chartreuse orchid blossoms, and exotic leaves would create peaceful studies of Earth, Water, and Fire.

Preppy. Low, wide cylindrical vases clad in a tasteful, pastel plaid fabric and finished with a simple bow, brimming with masses of green hydrangea, fragrant pink garden roses, unexpected, hot pink nerrine lilies, and finish with touches of chartreuse ladies mantle.

Glamorous. Luscious and sexy cattleya orchid blooms, gloriosa lilies, velvety roses, mokara orchids, and textured celosia designed with abandon in contemporary, black lacquer vases.

Garden. A winding, landscaped path of lacy, white alyssum would create a charming entrance to the tent. Collections of periwinkle agapanthus, pale blue scabiosa and delphinium, deep blue veronica and white Queen Anne's lace lends itself to the "just picked" look for a garden wedding. The flowers might be loosely gathered and placed into vintage mason jars.

Tables

You need tables for guests to gather. You need serving pieces to serve your meal. You need silverware to eat. You need plates and bowls to eat off of or out of. You need glasses to drink from. Chairs to sit on. And linens to make it all pretty. All of these elements fall into the category of table appointments.

You'll find rental tables in a variety of geometric sizes and shapes: rounds, squares, triangles, rectangles, half moons, and crescents in all different sizes. Creating combinations of shapes and sizes for a unique floor plan and unexpected seating arrangements is a wonderful way to express your style.

Develop a dynamic floor plan by checking off the arrangements that speak to you:

_____ Long, family-style tables for everyone to be close and
        talk

_____ Square tables that seat eight guests for more intimate
        groupings of couples

_____ A U-shaped arrangement of tables with you seated at the
        center

_____ Traditional twelve-seater tables set for ten, to provide
        comfortable room to eat

_____ A mix of rectangular and square tables, some seating
        eight, some seating ten, to allow seating of groups more
        naturally with one another

_____ Your ideas:

Some venues, such as hotels and clubs, provide the tables, china, stemware, chairs, and even house linens. What these venues offer may be right in line with the personality of your wedding. If not, rent a few key elements, such as tortoiseshell chargers, amber wine glasses, and a copper pin-tuck linen, to embellish the existing items the venue offers. With many venues, you will need to rent *all* of your table appointments, everything from the salt and pepper shakers to the coffee spoons and everything in between.

Since table groupings take up a serious amount of real estate in most of the floor plans for most of the weddings, there is an opportunity to create a major visual impact with your linen selection. Close your eyes and picture a neutral room and visualize twenty tables swathed in plain, white cotton-poly linens. Click the internal mouse in your mind and switch the linens to rich red velvet . . . then, to sage dupioni silk . . . then to shimmering platinum. The color and texture of your linen choice can be a defining element in relation to the personality of your venue.

Think about plain cotton-poly blends in a variety of colors, satins, silks and pin-tucks, damasks and hemstitched linens, gauzy overlays, embroidered overlays, and sparkle overlays. Linens studded with crystals or pearls. Stripes and plaids. Moroccan prints and Mexican serapes. Burlap. The color and fabric options seem endless. And, if that isn't enough, anything can be custom made. Even linen chair accessories such as sheer chair covers, chair jackets, chair ties, and chair tassels are also available through linen companies.

Some venues own chairs. If you like them and they work with your design concepts, by all means, use them. If you disdain them you have a couple of options. Most chairs can be covered with fabric chair covers or spruced up with chair ties. But this becomes a very specific look in and of itself. To be blunt, *dated* is the word that comes to mind. The other option is to rent chairs. Rental chairs range from simple wooden folding chairs to formal Versailles chairs to architectural fusion chairs to modern acrylic ghost chairs, to mention a few. Some rental companies' inventories include interchangeable cushions, so you have flexibility with your cushion color, as well.

With table appointments there are so many options to flirt with and so many opportunities to express your bridal style. The following is a style exploration applied to table appointments, much like it was applied to flowers. Remember, these are just starting points, to get you thinking.

Style Exploration: Tables

Classic. Using the club or hotel's existing tables, chairs, china, and linens and dressing them up with a few key rental items: sheer silver overlays detailed with a graceful smattering of hand-sewn crystal beading; silver beaded chargers; and mother-of-pearl silverware.

Zen. Large, square tables covered in tailored, white silk dupioni linens. White square plates, bamboo silverware, and contemporary Calvin Klein stemware create a clean, precise tabletop.

Preppy. A variety of tables such as cocktail tables, highboy tables, and forty-eight-inch round tables, establish a wonderful atmosphere to mix and mingle. Rolled napkins neatly banded with a plaid ribbon and white plates with tasteful bands of gold will be stacked at the buffet stations.

Glamorous. Serpentine or crescent-shaped tables winding their way through a reception, providing very unique seating for guests. The long, slinky tables could be dressed in red velvet and feature swanky red palette overlays. Tall, straight backs of the black fusion chairs outlined with red feather boas would add to the outrageous amount of texture and drama at these tables.

Garden. Homemade, periwinkle blue, seersucker table runners might add a welcome touch to the simplest of white cotton table cloths. White folding garden chairs and basic stemware, silverware, and white china could be in keeping with the style of this reception.

Lighting

You will be spending a lot of money on your reception to achieve your desired look. Lighting is the *lynch pin* to accomplishing your style goals. If you do not invest in some lighting, you are likely to be disappointed in the outcome.

Lighting can physically alter or shape a space more successfully than any other design element. This sentence is being repeated so that it really sinks in. *Lighting can physically alter or shape a space more successfully than any other design element.* It directs focus to the areas where you want your guests' attention and diverts focus from areas you don't want your guests to notice. Lighting also has the power to transform the color palette in a venue, add texture to plain expanses of ceiling or wall, highlight wonderful architectural details, and create mood.

What time of day is your reception?

Are there any windows?

How much of an effect will natural light have on the space?

Is it enough?

How long will it last?

Investigate existing lighting capabilities. Examine the dimmer options, the chandelier options, and what lights are on what circuits. Determine how much control you have over the existing lighting at your venue. Talk to your site contact or the building engineer to banter about possibilities. Make sure you visit the location during the time you've planned for your reception, preferably during the same season, and ideally, during an ongoing event.

What do you notice about the existing lighting?

Can you see the architectural details of your venue, or are they lost in shadow?

Is the art or sculpture in the venue illuminated?

Do you notice the flowers? Are the colors distinct?

Where are you going to make your grand entrance as Mr. and Mrs.? Will you make that entrance in light or shadow?

Pin-spot lighting offers a great deal of flexibility and direction with your lighting. A pin-spot light is a beam of light that is focused on a specific item or area. We recommend using pin spots to illuminate your centerpieces and the cake. If you have buffets or food stations, light those as well. The pin spots can also be used with a broader focus to illuminate the dance floor, the band, or the DJ. The pin-spot lighting is either accomplished through existing features or through bringing in lighting equipment and creating freestanding light trees.

If pin-spot lighting is not available or is out of your priorities range, up lights are a less expensive way to create ambience throughout the space. Up lights are exactly what they sound like, lights that focus their beam *up*. Any of these lights can be gelled in colors to enhance the look of the room. For example, you can use a rich amber gel to create more warmth, you can use a red gel for a hot, fiery look, or a blue gel for a cool look. Up lighting can illuminate columns, walls space, alcoves, windows, backdrops, and fabric panels, as well as flank entrances and exits. A combination of pin spots and up lights is a very worthwhile event investment.

Lighting is key to adding some true dimension and flair to an outdoor space, and when you make sure pathways are illuminated, you mind the safety of your guests. Up lights, luminaries, solar-powered path lights, lanterns, tiki torches, votive candles enclosed in glass bowls and dotted throughout an expanse of lawn, white Italian lights detailing tree branches and such will dramatically define the outdoor space.

Now that you're a bit more familiar with lighting options, take a look at them as they apply to style and design. Think about how your style of reception can be best illuminated.

Style Exploration: Lighting

Classic. Illuminate the tabletops and cake with pin spots. Washes of ambient light could highlight the dance floor and stage. Existing chandeliers and sconces in the venue may be dimmed to offer a warm, subtle glow throughout the room.

Zen. Up lights strategically placed underneath large areca palm trees can create dramatic leaf shadows on the ceiling and walls. This simple but effective lighting used throughout the space has transformative power.

Preppy. Washes of ambient light gelled with pink gels can create a rosy glow throughout this reception. A few up lights gelled with apple green placed around the perimeter of the room could establish a wonderful balance of these two prominent colors for a preppy reception.

Glamorous. Red and raspberry gels over the light fixtures establish a dramatic, color-saturated atmosphere. Up lights at the entrance, the stage backdrop, and the perimeter walls of the venue will continue the drama.

Garden. Votive candles enclosed in clear glass bowls dotted throughout an expanse of lawn and simple white paper bag luminaries lining pathways are wonderful ways to bring light into a garden wedding. Inside, several washes of light directed at the ceiling keep the atmosphere cheery and light.

Additional Style Opportunities

There are so many amazing ways to establish style and mood. Fabric, furniture, backdrops, props, and on, and on, and on. Listed below are a few more opportunities illustrated in context, much like we've done with the flowers, tablescapes, and lighting. This section offers a few more interesting ways to apply style to your wedding.

Classic: Imagine the entrance into the ballroom framed with a romantic, sheer ivory curtain detailed with lush, floral tiebacks.

Zen: Clean, spare and geometric describe the appropriate furniture for a few lounge groupings, including white leather couches and large, square glass coffee tables. Shoji screens are a great way to define the space around each grouping, as well as create a sense of intimacy within each grouping.

Preppy: A monogrammed dance floor might be perfect for the preppy couple. The monogram can be projected by light, or crafted out of a vinyl appliqué.

Glamorous: How about a two to three tiered stage just because it is so much *more?* The stage could be covered in red vinyl for a wet look. A backdrop of red velvet with sheer raspberry panels and bordered with red feather boas might act as the final show stopper.

Garden: Umbrella tables, or even large, free standing market umbrellas add definition to a garden wedding. At night, the underbelly of the umbrellas (say that three times fast) could be lit with white Italian lights.

Your Style Exploration

Now, you try it. Jot down the style categories for your reception that interest you, list your favorite adjectives for inspiration, and let your imagination run free with ideas for your flowers, tables, and lighting.

Style category/categories (a blend of several is terrific): _____

_____

Inspirational adjectives: _____

Flowers: _____

Tables: _____

Lighting: _____

Additional opportunities: _____

CHAPTER 11

The Menu

The moment has arrived! It's time for the food.

You'll have several menus for your individual wedding events, such as your rehearsal dinner, cocktail hour, reception, after-party, and morning-after bridal breakfast or brunch. Figuring out your bridal style for each is one of the most enjoyable tasks of the wedding planning. After all, this is the taste of your wedding, and guests say it's the food that pleases them most at any wedding. They also notice when a menu has been hand-picked to show the couple's style, history, and heritage.

Your first consideration with your menu is the time of day (dinner food for a nighttime wedding, for instance), and the next is how traditional you would like to be. For instance, if your caterer offers you eight appetizer choices, are you and your partner the traditional types who want shrimp cocktail, bacon-wrapped scallops, canapés, and chicken satay skewers—all staples of the pre-reception offerings for years—or do you want to transport your guests to another place and time with creative theme building, perhaps all Thai appetizers, or Mexican bites, with not a curled pink shrimp in sight?

Many couples also look to the restaurant industry to determine what's hot in five-star eateries or international fusion cuisines. For example, one couple built their cocktail party menu directly from the meal they enjoyed at Mixx, the restaurant in Atlantic City's Borgata resort and casino, during their first weekend getaway together. They served sushi, marinated beef flanks, tuna tartare, onion straws, and other dishes they enjoyed during "the weekend when we knew this was IT."

Before addressing your menu style, go back to chapter 1, and also chapters 3 and 4, to read over your initial responses to questions involving food and drinks. Your first reactions undoubtedly held your deepest wishes for a menu that reflects your favorite meals, the tastes of home, flavors that bring back memories. You'll answer some of those questions again here, as a way to get you to refine your style definitions:

What was the best meal you enjoyed together? Provide all details, including the appetizers you shared, where you were, etc.?

What were the first meals you cooked for one another?

What was the meal from your engagement, if there was one?

What are your favorite family meals, your parents' specialties, holiday meals, celebratory meals?

Of all the cultural cuisines around the world, which are your favorites?

Are you connected to your own heritage? What dishes from your cultural background do you love?

List the top three dishes from your heritage and the top three dishes from your partner's heritage . . .

His   **Hers**

1. _____   1. _____

2. _____   2. _____

3. _____   3. _____

Which dishes did you really enjoy at other weddings or family celebrations?

Which traditional bridal dishes do you not want at your wedding?

Thinking seasonally for your wedding date, what are some menu items you can add to your list?

Which foods do you think of when you hear the word delectable? Choose a word to describe your bridal style so far, then write down the first five dishes that fit the theme.

What are your favorite comfort foods?

Your favorite cold foods?

Are you indulgent eaters, or health conscious?

Building Your Menu

Taste is an entirely exclusive thing. You are the only one in the world who can communicate your menu style. It is as individual as a fingerprint. Everyone has their own favorite dishes, meals that remind them of times in their love story, deeply ingrained family meal memories, favorite dishes from vacation. And these, not just standard listings on a caterer's checklist sheet, may play a large part in determining your menu style.

Is there a theme you wish you could use for your wedding, but the scope and size makes it impossible? You can do it at your cocktail party, on a smaller scale, yet still adding the flavor and tone you have dreamed of. Your wedding is an *experience* for both you and your guests, built around your sense of style. You'll get yet another chance at this party-sculpting when you think about your after-party . . . another chance to use your style and backgrounds to plan another unforgettable personalized celebration to your day.

Menu Styles

Here are some sample descriptions of menu styles to get you thinking about what will work best for you. Circle anything that sounds perfect for your evolving menu style and mention these ideas to your caterer. Use these descriptions together with all of your answers on the previous pages to custom-build your shared style, or combine your two different styles into an ideally blended expression of your tastes.

Traditional. Let other couples dream up Moroccan fantasies . . . you've long been dreaming of the iconic wedding dishes, such as lobster and filet mignon, chicken marsala, seared tuna with pineapples and mangoes, seafood bars . . . very traditional choices prepared in classic style.

Traditional with a Twist. A traditional menu can be accented with elements of your own personal style, heritage, or favorite dishes, such as a pierogi bar to pay homage to your Ukrainian or Polish heritage. These special dishes are like a painter's flourish, a bit of personalized color and flavor and texture to the palette of your traditional menu.

Contemporary and Trendy. Borrow what the celebrities are doing! Look at the websites of popular celebrity dinner spots, or even visit a few of the restaurants, if possible. Wolfgang Puck's Oscar parties menu is always featured on the website for the Oscars, so golden-carpet your menu with a few of his choices tailored to your style.

Fusion. Working with your caterer, you'll take two different menu styles and blend them together so well that your guests will think that Portuguese food has always been paired with Japanese food.

Cultural. The big trend is pulling dishes from your families' heritage—or even dishes from a culture you have visited or enjoy without being born into the lineage—and building or accenting your menu with those tasty touches.

Seasonal. If you'll have an autumn or winter wedding, especially in a phenomenal location such as a ski lodge or bed-and-breakfast with mood-setting views that have transported your guests to a new world, your menu may reflect some of the local seasonal flavors. A soup bar may be de rigueur for your winter wedding, or you may pull in acorn squash or pumpkin tartlets, fall game meats, and more options that your caterer can suggest. At one winter wedding, coconut-crusted shrimp was designed and presented on an ice platter as "snowball shrimp," and honeyed ham was the perfect replacement for a prime rib at the carving station.

Green/Organic. You feel strongly that your healthy lifestyle should come into play at your reception by using local organic produce, and so forth, but you still want to please your guests' palates. So your menu style is true to your tastes and integrity, yet the creativity of the dishes still thrills those who think chicken fried steak is a delicacy.

Service Style

The next level of determining your menu style is figuring out the best *presentation* of the foods you'll provide. You may think that passed-around hors d'oeuvres are the essence of elegant serving style at your cocktail party, while a lengthy buffet table says "potluck" or "family reunion" to you. For each wedding event, think about how your guests will receive your tasty choices:

At the Sit-Down Meal

- *American style*—Also called seated style or sit-down style, it's the traditional style of each guest being served an individual dish that has been plated in the kitchen.

- *French style*—Platters of food are prepared and served tableside, such as with Dover sole, carved rack of lamb, or crepes Suzette.
- *Russian style*—Waiters wear white gloves as they walk around with platters and use a fork and spoon to serve each guest a portion of the entrée, starch, and vegetable as directed.
- *Family style*—Platters and bowls of food are set in the middle of the table, and guests are free to fill their own plates.
- *"Gaucho" style*—An international style of meat service where servers called "gauchos" walk around with large portions of beef on a big skewer, and carve the juicy meat right onto guests' plates.
- *Buffet style*—Dinner is served in a buffet arrangement, with guests walking the line and visiting stations.

*Answer this question: A couple who chooses traditional wedding food is*_____
_____

When you think about the menu for your wedding, what do you want your guests to remember as being truly reflective of your relationship and style? _____
_____
_____

CHAPTER 12

The Sweet Stuff

W hen you think *bridal style*, the wedding gown might be the first image you have, but surely your wedding cake is also at the top of your list. Wedding cake styles range from the classic fairy tale, ultratraditional, five-tier, white-frosted masterpiece that's featured in so many bridal magazines to brightly colored, whimsical, even "tilted" cake styles that seem to come right out of a children's book. Anything goes when it comes to your cake style, and given the artistry and vision of today's cake designers, you can request *anything* in *any* style.

Your goal here, then, is to refine your vision—perhaps for the first time venturing away from the storybook cake design of piped white frosting on that five-tiered cake covered with sugar-frosting roses and pipettes. You might think . . . *chocolate* . . . or Tiffany-blue boxes . . . a cake designed to emulate the Taj Mahal or the Eiffel Tower . . . a pyramid dusted with real edible gold . . . even a bright orange cake piped to match the lace design of your gown.

In a very real sense, your edible cake begins with an incredible exploration of your style.

The wonderful news is that you don't have to match your wedding cake style to the formality and style of your wedding. Though it sounds counterintuitive, today's wedding freedoms mean that it's *your* style that comes through in your "cake statement." So even at the most formal, elegant wedding, the centerpiece of the room—the focal point—might be a brightly colored pink and brown cake with pink flowers and pink ribbons around the base of each layer . . . and ethereal pink butterflies on ultra-thin wire sticking out of the top layer. The cake is so *you* . . . a perfect touch of modern color and your favorite butterflies. And it works perfectly with the formality of your wedding. So ignore any of those old online articles that say you *must* have a formal cake, iced in traditional design or covered with a cascade of fresh flowers. Your cake style is limited only by your imagination . . . and then further refined by your cake designer's expertise.

You've generated dozens of buzzwords throughout the first chapters of this book. See how they inform your style definitions in flavors, textures, shapes, and patterns. All apply to your cake and additional desserts. And the groom's cake? Just another chance to express your style. In fact, some couples are setting out the extra cake, but designating it not as the groom's cake, but rather as the couple's cake. Their main wedding cake is elegant and traditional, as they wish it to be, but the couple's cake is a constructed and colorful depiction of the couple's love of travel or sports or their favorite season, a city-chic cake to convey their love of metropolitan nightlife, or even a Fudgie the Whale ice cream cake to pay homage to their childlike, playful relationship.

So for both of these cakes, read through the style descriptions here, circle the words you love, write in your additional inspirations, and communicate this information to your cake designer. But first, use the space below to record your takes on wedding cakes you've loved and loathed in the past.

> *The wedding and family celebration cakes we have loved: (Note: use lots of descriptions on flavors and textures here, such as "the tangy taste of blackberries" and "the crunch of walnuts"—this is a key source for language to use with your cake designer.)*

> *The wedding and family celebration cakes we have hated:*

Exploring Your Wedding Cake Style

Your Cake's Personality

Here are some descriptions and examples of the kinds of cakes that fit with the different styles you've already explored—and perhaps decided on—throughout this book. Look through all of them, even if you've fallen in love with one particular style for the other elements of your wedding plans, since inspiration has a way of coming at you from a different direction. A description in "whimsical," for instance, might be the perfect touch for your groom's cake. Or a blended element into a traditional cake.

Traditional. The five-tier white cake, frosted with frothy swirls and icing roses. It's the storybook cake, gorgeous in its simplicity, separated by columns or with layers stacked directly on top of one another, perhaps topped with a traditional bride and groom cake topper or a cascade of fresh, colorful or monochromatic white flowers for an all-natural, ultrabridal look.

Traditional with a Twist. The traditional cake description, but iced with decorative swirls. Perhaps you've asked for sugar-paste flowers in a color scheme, marzipan fruits, or sugar-paste birds or butterflies. Your cake layers might feature a colored ribbon wrapped around each base, with a spray of flowers (real or icing-made), and your cake baker might swirl your monogram onto the front layer of the cake.

Contemporary. Your cake layers are covered perfectly with rolled fondant for that smooth wrapped look. The fondant might be white, or in blush or bright colors, with rolled fondant strips designed to look like a ribbon bow. With expertly placed icing, you've designed a swirls or lattice design, pipette dotted accents, or intricate pearl-type details on the ribbon tie. Contemporary cakes are not always made of round concentric layers. Your cake may be layers of ovals or squares, or even triangles as the new trend conveys.

Casual. A chocolate-frosted cake with pink ribbons wrapped around the base of each layer, or a simpler two-tier frosted cake in white or blush pink, cascading or dotted with fresh flowers. A single-layer sheet cake might be your choice for an outdoor casual wedding, punctuated by a border of daisy blossoms, finished with a hand-picked bouquet of fresh daisies sprouting from the top.

Cultural. Your cake is an accent to the room's décor, a gem, an exotic focal point. Use your heritage's colors and patterns, such as a red and yellow Chinese palette with symbols iced onto the cake.

Whimsical. Think about a cake that would sit on the tea table in *Alice in Wonderland*. Each layer is covered with a different shade of rolled fondant in bright, primary colors, with large dots of colorful icing. The newest look and the intended effect is to tilt the layers so that the cake appears to be melting off the table. Other whimsical cakes might be a fun themed cake featuring your favorite sports team, or brightly colored layers studded with contrasting or coordinating quarter-size fondant circles and stars on wire stickpins, coordinated with the same shapes and colors icing-attached to the tops and sides of all cake layers. A bright pink wedding cake might be wire-stickpinned with ethereal butterfly accents that seem to be floating all around the cake.

All-Natural. A simply frosted cake set on a bed of greenery, with greenery and fresh flowers accenting the cake. A border of bright green wheat grass around the bottom layer of the cake might contrast the lighter sage green icing color, with white icing swirls. Another vision: the robin's egg blue wedding cake with a faux nest on top filled with white doves or lovebirds.

Architectural. How did they do *that*? Separated by unique pedestals, your architectural cake features different shapes, such as a square base with a circular middle layer, and a smaller pyramid on top (all secured with a thick wooden dowel through the middle and hidden from sight). Or cake layers presented atop varying heights of Lucite platforms, each layer a unique shape, size, and possibly hue. A slanted pyramid might be your choice for architectural cake design, or a replica of the Taj Mahal or

Leaning Tower of Pisa. Some couples who met at landmarks often choose that site as the theme for their wedding cakes.

And let's not forget that you can select many different styles of mini wedding cakes, placing them in the centers of each guest table. Clever cake bakers have designed coordinating yet different two-layer cakes in frosted or fondant designs, as mini wedding cakes in a traditional model, or cakes to look like snow globes or wrapped gifts complete with fondant ribbons. Cake bakers' artistry is unlimited. Your style comes from what you consider a bridal cake.

Fillings and Frostings

We encourage you to thoroughly explore your cake baker's possibility lists for fillings and frostings, looking for the unique flavors that call out to you or remind you of a key moment in your relationship. Perhaps you were out at dinner sharing a cannoli when you knew this was The One. As such, you can select a wedding cake with a cannoli filling. We couldn't possibly categorize any cake flavors or fillings as fitting into any particular style . . . this one is all yours to explore.

So think about the fillings and frostings that say "home" to you. Which say "decadence"? Which say "natural"? "trendy"? "exotic"? Record your thoughts here or in your Possibilities Notebook for discussion with your cake designer.

Additional Desserts

Again, your choice of additional desserts for your wedding events—both reception and rehearsal dinner, as well as your wedding weekend events—depends upon your wedding's theme and formality, your personalities, the history of your love story, and your favorite tastes and indulgences. For you, a cake and chocolate-covered strawberries (the *big* ones!) might be the perfect style for you, or you may want to go with the full Viennese table covered with a buffet of cakes, pies, mousses, and tartlets. So we'll leave you to your own inspirations as you fill in the desserts that fit in to your version of style. Need some ideas? Visit your favorite bakery.

All of this consideration of your food style has probably made you thirsty. Or at least thinking about food and wine pairings, since the two are inextricably linked. You're about to move on to a tasty next step in determining your bridal style . . .

CHAPTER 13

The Drink Menu

Of all the wedding categories, the drink menu is the *newest* realm where brides and grooms wish to express their style, personalities, and their history as a couple. Of course, there's always a sentimental touch when a couple serves the same vintage of wine or champagne that they shared upon their engagement, or the same vintages served at their parents' weddings, but this goes beyond sentiment. Whereas wedding couples in the past didn't delve into the style of their toasting champagne or their drink menu—they simply pointed to a package list for "top shelf," "mid-shelf," or "house" wines and liquors—the trend for today is to create an unmistakable style imprint for all the drinks offered at the wedding.

Start with the following intake questions, blend in your earlier answers in chapter 1, and you'll further refine your images and ideals in as much detail as possible, even words that are surprising to you:

What is your favorite celebratory drink when you get terrific news? A glass of champagne? A fine wine? A frozen margarita?

Describe the three most unforgettable drinks you ever had while on vacation.

1. _____

2. _____

3. _____

What was the best drink you ever had at a restaurant?

What kind of wine do you choose for important client dinners or entertaining at home?

What kind of wine or champagne do you give as gifts?

Do you have a dream vintage of champagne or wine?

What is the most refreshing nonalcoholic drink you've ever had?

You've just recalled not only your favorite drinks, but the memories and emotions associated with them. That unforgettable bellini you enjoyed during a vacation to Sanibel Island could become a part of your bridal brunch drink menu, because you want that event to convey the same kind of relaxation and freshness, sweetness and sunny sense of escape that you found on Sanibel. That phenomenal pinot you gave to your boss for her birthday, and to your parents for their anniversary, chosen for its rich depth and smoothness, an inspired feeling of "the good life" . . . that could be on your wedding reception bar card. It's indulgent, with a hint of cherry. Just one taste of it, and you're back in Sonoma.

Why have your drink menu reflect your bar manager's style—

or worse, no personal style at all—when it could reflect *your* style?

Best of all, *you don't have to choose just one style.*

Seasonal Style

You might think that the formality and theme of your wedding would be the first place we start, but we're going right to the calendar. The date of your wedding, the season of your wedding, will be the first, foundational defining aspect of your drink style. For instance, summer drinks are light, fruity, refreshingly cool, brightly colored in citrus yellows and oranges, frosty, tropical, fresh, "beachy," such as piña coladas, daiquiris, sangrias.

Fall and winter drinks are warm or hot, spiced, creamy, smooth, chocolaty, cinnamon-touched, reminiscent of a ski lodge or warming relief by the fireplace after a long day of sledding and snowball fights.

Go back to your answers in chapter 3, The Four Seasons. The perfect drinks may be listed there . . .

What is the season of your wedding, and which adjectives or descriptions suit the drinks that come to mind for you?

Are You Traditional or Trendy?

Picture a crystal flute of champagne. Imagine every aspect of it, from the glass to the color of the champagne, the pearl-like strings of bubble paths rising from the bottom to the top of the glass. What color did you see? Traditional pale yellow, or blush pink, peach, ruby grapefruit red? Obviously, a traditionalist will see what we so subtly call "traditional pale yellow," while a trendier, more creative and color-based type will see their champagne splashed with raspberry, peach, or pomegranate juice . . . perhaps with a few berries or fine slices of peach at the bottom of the glass for a visual element and unexpected flavor and texture.

Let's do the same with a martini. What are you picturing? A straight-up, clear liquid in a traditional martini glass with two olives on the spear? Or a neon blue martini that makes a sapphire look dark and dull? A bright green appletini? A chocolate brown espresso martini with rich cocoa powder dusting the rim?

The color and "twist" of your chosen drinks depends on your style: traditional or trendy, classic or creative/colorful/kicky, timeless or "time for Last Call."

When you speak to a bar manager, you'll get an understanding nod and a personalized bar card flip-through when you can say, "We prefer the traditional servings of our drinks, classic and timeless takes on the martini, sidecar, Manhattan . . . like a 1930s lounge in the Golden Age of Hollywood." That description alone tells the bar manager the style of your menu, which mixed drinks to provide in which types of glasses (traditional highball, traditional martini), with which types of garnishes (twist of lemon, two olives).

Your nontraditional, creative, irreverent style might be conveyed to your bar manager like this: "We love the traditional drinks—martinis, sidecars, Manhattans—but we want a more modern twist on them, bright colors, something unexpected. Where most people would do apple martini, we want a Girl Scout Cookie taste with mint and chocolate, something that our guests will immediately recognize as tastes from their youth." Or: "We want tropical drinks, but the usual piña colada is a little too boring. We're thinking a mix of mango, raspberry, coconut, and some Cointreau for a sweeter taste that transports them to the islands." You don't have to be an expert in what to mix, you just need to express what you're going for. The bar manager heard "tropical . . . not boring . . . mango, raspberry, coconut . . . Cointreau . . . the islands." He'll have the rum out before you know it, along with additional select flavors to custom-create drinks for you.

Wedding Drinks

Here is where you'll create your list of the perfect drink offerings for your reception.

Designing Your Drink Selection

Martinis

They're the top trend in wedding drinks. Here you'll find real martinis broken down into a sample of personality and style matchups. (Look back at the styles listed in chapter 1, and see if one calls to you.):

Your Style and Personality	*Martinis to Match You*
Traditional, Classic	*Classic martini:* vodka/gin, dry vermouth, lemon twist or olive garnish

Your Style and Personality	*Martinis to Match You*
Traditional, Classic	*Classic Manhattan:* bourbon/whiskey, sweet vermouth, cherry
	Dirty martini: gin/vodka, dry vermouth, olive juice, olive garnish
	Gibson: gin/vodka, pearl onion garnish
	Sidecar: Hennessey, Cointreau, sour mix, lime
City-Chic, New York, Contemporary	*Cosmopolitan:* vodka with citrus, Cointreau, cranberry juice, lime juice, lime twist
	Appletini: vodka with apple liqueur
	Lemontini: vodka, lemon juice, sugar, Sprite, served in a sugar-rimmed glass
	Blue sapphire: Bombay Sapphire, blue Curaçao, dry vermouth, lemon twist
	Espresso martini: vodka, Kahlua, and espresso

Your Style and Personality	*Martinis to Match You*
	Cappuccino martini: vodka, Godiva liqueur, cappuccino liqueur
Caribbean, Exotic, Island	*Key West martini:* orange-flavored vodka, Malibu rum, Midori, peach schnapps, cranberry juice, lime garnish
	Mango cosmopolitan: vodka, mango juice, triple sec, cranberry juice
	Watermelon martini: kurant, watermelon juice, cranberry juice
Sophisticated, Romantic	*Champagne cocktail:* champagne, sugar, dash of bitters
	Bellinitini: vodka, peach puree, peach schnapps, champagne

Your Style and Personality	*Martinis to Match You*
Whimsical, Eclectic	*Almond Joy:* vodka, rum, amaretto
	Creamsicle: vodka, Stoli, Licor 43, orange juice, and cream
	Tootsie Roll: orange-flavored vodka, Godiva liqueur, Grand Marnier

These are just a few of the vast array of specialty, creative martinis out there, so talk to the bar manager about choosing the perfect flavors to suit your style.

Mixed Drinks

What's your style in mixed drinks? More often than not, a wedding drink menu will contain the "usuals": Jack and coke, vodka and cranberry juice, and so on. There is not as much "styling" with these as you'll find with champagne and martinis, so it's your call whether to stick with the bar manager's offerings or add a twist to the usuals with presentation style. To that vodka and cranberry juice, you might ask them to add slices of lime cut into a fan shape, rather than a wedge. Or incorporate star fruit slices, which is so beautiful and *un*usual. Or, serve the drinks in glasses of unexpected size, shape, or color.

Your glassware, too, can add a splash of style to an "old standard," such as traditional martinis served in cobalt blue martini glasses, or red glasses with zigzag stems. Visit www.tableware today.com for a look at the newest in mixed-drink glasses—the shading, glass bubbles blown into the bases, textures, fabulous stems, and colored rims. It may be your taste to serve a standard or exotic drink in a glass that displays your fabulous style sense, or works with your wedding's theme.

And don't forget the style opportunities with a pitcher of sangria. Those gorgeous, jewel-colored pitchers of fruity wine can be a centerpiece all their own with the addition of bountiful slices of apple and orange, lime and lemon. Some bartenders also include bright rounds of blood orange or ruby red grapefruit for artistry as well as taste. These cultural pitchers become a part of the table's décor with color to match the bridesmaids' dresses. The same goes for mojitos, with their pale green color and minty inserts.

Would you like to match your drink colors to your décor, to your bridesmaids' dress colors, to the flowers in the centerpieces or bouquets, to rose petals scattered on the bridal white tablecloths?

Here, record the colors you've chosen for your wedding and brainstorm color-coordinating drinks to add to your bar menu . . .

1. _____

2. _____

3. _____

4. _____

Wines

The rule with wines is to match them to the flavors of the food you'll serve, pairing the perfect bouquet with the flavors of your meats, poultry, seafood, and sauces. If you're not already familiar with the rules and wish to be educated before you sit down with your bar manager, visit www.winespectator.com for complete wine/food pairing charts and the latest news on vintages getting the best rating from experts today.

As for communicating your wishes to your bar manager, complete the following exercise, with a look back to the questions you've already answered in your intake questionnaire and other sections throughout the book.

Do you like wine? Why?

Do you prefer red or white? Why?

Read the labels on your favorite wine bottles. What words do you see?

Some bottles feature important keywords like "round, intense cherry; plum tartness; supple oak flavors; elegant creaminess"; "ripe aromas of black cherry, vanilla, and a hint of spice followed by cherry, jammy berry, and black tea–infused flavors"; "silky smooth texture, finishes very soft and delicate." Write down any phrases or descriptions that speak to your five senses. When you sit down with your bar manager, you'll then be able to express exactly the taste style you desire.

Record your wine description here:

Of course, you can select the same vintages that have been a part of your love story—the wine from your first date, the wine you shared on a special vacation, the wine from a country you love or the country of your heritage—and we encourage you to add your style in that manner. Tell your story.

Beers

There was a time when brides declared, "There will be no beer at the wedding!" However, today's beers have gotten a makeover, a styling of their own to fit in well at even formal weddings. You'll always see good domestic and imported beers on wedding drink menus, and now the bride and groom are extending their personal style choices into beers, brews, lagers, and ales. The advent of seasonal beers and microbrew beers presents an opportunity to affix a style stamp as you offer unique beers and microbrews at the wedding. Don't forget the range of summer ales and cider ales that would match the season of your wedding.

What does your beer say about your style?

After-Dinner Drinks

Are you the cognac type? Is it your definition of sophistication to swirl that rich, cinnamon-colored liqueur in a snifter? Or are you the type to lift a pinkie while sipping a cappuccino? Do you love the mint drizzle on top of an Irish coffee? Your own favorite after-dinner drinks—perhaps just a splash of Bailey's Irish Cream in your coffee—that you enjoy on special nights out will determine your style of after-dinner drinks for your wedding. Cognac, brandy, Chambord . . . the list goes on.

> *When you've enjoyed these night-enders in the past, what feelings did you associate with them?*

> *What's the social connection of after-dinner drinks? Do they remind you of family memories?*

Nonalcoholic Drinks

Iced tea and lemonade evoke the charm of the South. A fruity punch with frothy sorbet on top says *playful party*. Virgin daiquiris provide an island celebration without the hangover. Pitchers of ice water with lemon say natural and pristine refreshment. A root beer float is a fun throwback to childhood and perhaps a great addition to a dessert hour. Think about your favorite soft drinks and iced teas, associating memories with them, and list them here:

1. _____

2. _____

> *Use your Possibilities Notebook to record your additional drinks notes, and include any advertisements or drink recipes you see in magazines.*

Many guests say the menu and drinks are the centerpiece of a successful wedding, but you'll hear from plenty of experienced wedding-goers that the *entertainment* is as important as a really butter-soft chateaubriand or a fine champagne. So switch your mind-set from gourmand to guitar, from dining to dancing, and get ready to define your music and entertainment styles . . .

CHAPTER 14

Entertainment

Music sets a mood. The key to your wedding music and entertainment style is not only about what you want to *hear*, but how you want to *feel*—and want your guests to feel—during the ceremony, cocktail hour, reception, and after-party.

So take notes on the details of each party. What's your desired mood for each portion of your wedding day celebration?

	Ceremony	*Cocktails*	*Reception*	*After-Party*
Season				
Day of the Week				
Time of Day				
Number of Guests				
Format of Cocktails & Reception				

	Ceremony	*Cocktails*	*Reception*	*After-Party*
Style of Venue				
Age Range of Your Guests				
Ratio of Locals to Out-of-Towners				
Ratio of Family to Friends				
Desired Mood				

Remember, you get to set different tones throughout your wedding.

Here are some descriptions to get you thinking, to connect with styles for each phase of your wedding day, and even for the celebratory days before the wedding, and at breakfast or brunch on the morning after. You get to set different musical tones throughout your wedding weekend, so your ceremony may be classical entertainment, your cocktail hour may be smoky jazz, your reception all club music or Motown, your after-party all Michael Bublé and Tony Bennett, and your morning-after brunch can go back to classical. Here are some examples to start you off:

- Classic mixed with the natural, like Sting's concert tour in Tuscany

- Simple and lyrics based, like John Mayer's acoustic performances
- Moving, like Andrea Bocelli's pure voice
- Velvety, like Nina Simone or Etta James
- Fun and retro, like the soundtrack from the musical *Jersey Boys* or Motown
- Instrumental and airy, like R. Carlos Nakai's Native American flute music
- Rhythmic and moving, like African drummers
- Joyful, like Louis Armstrong's "What a Wonderful World"
- Regal, like harp or cello music

What comes to mind for you?

-
-
-
-
-
-

Use this collection of keywords and music styles to help uncover your entertainment preferences. This chart of musical and thematic styles, along with the detailed information above, will give you a tremendous head start in communicating with your wedding coordinator, your band, or your DJ.

We'd like our ceremony/cocktail hour/reception/after-party to be . . .

	Ceremony	*Cocktails*	*Reception*	*After-Party*
A capella				
Bluegrass				
Blues				
Celebratory				
Classic				
Club				
Country				
Culture-Specific (list the culture)				
Era-Specific (list the era)				
Exuberant				
Festive/Fun				
Gospel				
Humorous				

	Ceremony	*Cocktails*	*Reception*	*After-Party*
Inspiring				
Intimate				
Instrument- Specific (list instruments)				
Jammin'				
Jazz				
Joyful				
Light				
MoTown				
Moving				
Musician- Specific (list musician or band)				
Night-Life				
Region- Specific (list region)				
Rat Pack				

	Ceremony	Cocktails	Reception	After-Party
Regal				
Religious				
Retro				
Rock 'n' Roll				
Rock-a-Billy				
Rhythmic				
Sacred				
Smoky				
Sophisticated				
Spiritual				
Traditional				
Uplifting				
World Music				

For some couples, the entertainment is their highest priority. So they choose their location and décor, menu and favors, flowers and invitations based on their style of music and tone. For instance, one couple from Cincinnati knew that they wanted 1920s-era music and a flapper theme for their wedding, so they searched for a Great Gatsby–esque mansion where they would hold their wedding. They envisioned their music and entertainers as the base for their plan. When asked to define their bridal style, they used the words, "back in time," "Gatsby-esque," and "white tent by the pool." They envisioned their guests all in white, and the bride wanted to wear a flapper dress. All based on the music they loved from that era.

Return to your earlier answers in chapters 1 and 4 to see what surfaced in your sense memories to sound. See what seeds were planted that relate to your entertainment. Then continue on with these personal style questions:

Would you like your entertainment to transport you to another place or time? (The feeling of a favorite vacation? Your childhood home? Your college days?)

What are your expectations and/or concerns for a band or orchestra at a wedding?

What are your expectations and/or concerns for a DJ at a wedding? (Do you prefer original versions of songs, by the recording artists who made them famous, or do you like the unique touch of a band or live performer? Remember, you can have original artists' renditions at some wedding events, and live performances at others.)

What is your style when it comes to band versus DJ?

Do you love the unexpected? At every family wedding, there has been a pianist at the ceremony and a live band at the reception, so would it be more *you* to have a guitarist at the ceremony and cultural singers and dancers at the reception? Many couples want their receptions to be the equivalent of their guests going out to a night at the theater, a real performance that widens their eyes and gets them clapping. Club music with the deep bass . . . that might not be for you. Harp music might remind you of a tea party attended by grandmothers in white lace gloves. Steel drum music might transport you right to the islands, even though you couldn't pull off an island destination wedding.

Special Dances

Your first dance. The father-daughter and mother-son dances. Dances with kids, and with the bridal party. Will you go traditional with the spotlight dances, the back-and-forth slow dance as everyone watches, or would you like a choreographed tango with each other, a waltz with your father, a family-tradition polka with your mother? Do you envision a Klezmer band with all of your guests dancing an exhilarating hora? Anything is possible. It's up to you to define it all.

PART FIVE

Essentials

Chapter 15

Invitations, Programs, Place Cards, and More

The fact that invitation design etiquette has changed so much in the past few years, allowing you far more freedom for both formal and informal invitations and other printed items, gives you a whole new world of style options. So whatever your preconceptions about what a proper invitation has to be, throw them out the window. You're now free to design invitations and matching or coordinating additional print items that suit you, the style and location of your wedding, your favorite quote or poetry, even a photo of the two of you. You're no longer bound to the formal white or ecru minimalist single panel card with the black italic lettering . . . unless you wish to be.

Save-the-Date Cards

This is the first piece of wedding stationery that your guests see, so the style and color conveys a lot about you both as a couple, and perhaps what your wedding will be like. We say "perhaps" because many couples send these all-important calendar block reservers a year ahead of the wedding—particularly if the event will be held during busy summer months or vacation times—and they might not know the actual colors and style of the wedding yet. So go with something fun and colorful, as you'll find a wide range of cards and font styles out there, and include the most important information with flair: the date, time, and place of the wedding; your *full* names (for those faraway relatives and friends who have a lot of contacts with your same first names); and your personalized wedding website URL. You can use the back of the card to say where you're registered, and also hotel reservation information.

Then send these out at least six months before the wedding date.

Your Invitations Package

"It's important to select a design that is reflective of your own personal style," says Dominique Schurman, owner of Papyrus (www.papyrusonline.com). "The invitation is the first glimpse into your special day that your guests will have. It's important to remember the invitation sets the tone for the entire day."

STYLE DESIGN FROM NEILLE

Our first meeting with a client is really a "getting to know you" time. We discuss all of the details and their existing thoughts about their envisioned wedding. We always ask about how they met, and how the groom proposed. Many

*times these key conversations have been the basis for the de-
signs we create. One couple had been living around the corner from each other for almost a year and had never crossed
paths. Their theme, then, was "Love was just around the
corner." We created the invitations suite using the bride's favorite colors—eggplant paper with silver ink! Another couple
shared their proposal story in which the groom planned an
elaborate dinner out with champagne and flowers but knew
he may be too emotional when it came time to pop the question. Instead, he created a "love letter" he had the waitress
deliver. Their invite included four tiny little envelopes with
"Love Letters" in them.*

—Neille Hoffman, Aurum Design, www.aurumdesign.com

Here are the style concepts that will help you define your print
package style for your communication with your invitation experts. These concepts are also for your own clarity if you'll create
your own invitations, Save-the-Date cards, programs, place cards,
and all other print items for your big day:

Traditional Formal

Color: White or ecru card stock with black lettering

Panel style: Single panel

Shape: Rectangle or square

Graphics and borders: May include delicate flourishes, fleur-
de-lis, monogram or delicate single-line black borders, or
blush-colored pearlized borders

Wording flair: Adheres strictly to the traditional wording rules (see feature on page 210)

Personality: Elegant, classic, traditional

Inserts: Match the same color and font as the invitation, may have smaller monogram or flourish to match the set

Nontraditional Formal

Color: Any color from white or ecru to pastels to brights: red, blue, green, orange. Font may be in color to coordinate with card stock, such as bright bold red on a white card stock or a deeper hunter green on a sage green card stock. Any solid color goes. Dominique Schurman says, "Metallic or 'shiny papers' are another option to update the look."

Panel style: Single panel or dual-fold

Shape: Rectangle, square, oval, circle

Graphics and borders: Brighter colors in graphics and borders, perhaps a quarter-inch border in a solid color or border of daisy prints, colored monogram, color photo, or theme shape graphic on front cover of dual-fold invitation or at top of single panel invitation; invitation may have a ribbon bow at the top, with or without theme charm attached.

Wording flair: Still adheres to traditional wording style. May include RSVP at bottom of the card, which the ultratraditional invitation does not have.

Personality: Traditional, yet bright and eye catching, conveys the location of the invitation such as a seafoam green or aquamarine blue for a beach wedding.

Inserts: Inserts may match formal style, font and colors of invitation, or they may be on same color card stock with a coordinating color font to set inserts apart from invitation style. Example: pink card with red lettering for invite, inserts are pink cards with deeper pink lettering.

Trendy

Color: At the time of this printing, the hot colors are orange, brown, turquoise, and pinks, with combinations of blue and chocolate brown, and pink and chocolate brown leading the way at present.

Panel style: Single panel, dual-fold, scroll, booklet, origami

Shape: Rectangle, square, oval, circle, triangle, scalloped-edge rectangle or square, heart-shaped, origami fold-outs

Graphics and borders: Coordinating color stripes, paisleys, circles of color in corners or throughout, fun and trendy graphics like martini glasses or artists' renderings of the couple, color graphics from your digital camera, colored printings of your first names at the top and bottom corners of your invitation; not-so-subtle watermarks created by your graphics software; borders may be thicker stripes of color, cut-outs like hearts or stars, textured strips of fabric or faux-fur, ribbon ties with charm, even scrapbooking supply strips of textured shapes.

Wording flair: Departs from the traditional invitation script to show some personality. "We're getting married!" in gorgeous font across the top of the invitation. Incorporate the most important etiquette elements, such as your parents' names if they're hosting, and feel free to include a hint as to dress code: "Leave the stilettos at home! We'll be on the beach!"

Personality: Excitement, festive, colorful, ebullience, personalized, modern

Inserts: In coordinating colors with matching or coordinating fonts. Wording may be less formal as well, to match the style of the invitation.

City-Chic

Color: Red, Tiffany blue, silver and blue, chocolate and blue or pink, oranges

Panel style: Single-panel, dual-fold, tri-fold, or booklet

Shape: Rectangle, square (the favorite for this style), circle or oval, or cut to look like a Tiffany box

Graphics and borders: Chic and stylish graphics and colorful borders, flourishes and monograms, digital camera graphics or line drawing graphics reminiscent of a fashion designer's sketches, your names in big, calligraphy lettering. The invitation is often packaged like a gift, with a ribbon wrap and charm or buckle securing it.

Wording flair: May be traditional script, or incorporate "city-talk" such as mentioning martinis or champagne on the rooftop overlooking the cityscape.

Personality: Energetic, fabulous, trendy, exorbitant, nightlife, brights

Inserts: Match or coordinate with the invitation style. Some couples include a prefavor: a gift card to the spa in the hotel where the wedding will be held, invitations to additional wedding weekend events, cocktail parties, shows and tours.

Natural

Color: Beige, sage green, sky or sea blue, with deeper colors in the font. "Handmade papers are also commonly used," says Dominique Schurman of Papyrus. "These specialty papers incorporate elements from nature, such as actual leaves or petals."

Panel style: Single panel or dual-fold (to keep paper use to a minimum)

Shape: Rectangular, square, or oval

Graphics and borders: Elements of nature, such as leaves, ferns, seashells, sea horses, trees, butterflies, waterfalls, fields of tulips on the cover, florals, willow trees

Wording flair: Sticks to traditional wording script, with optional wording to convey outdoor location: "Join us as the sun sets over our ceremony at the botanical garden."

Personality: Fresh, natural, floral, greenery, lush, organic, lovely, back-to-nature

Inserts: Match the style of the invitation, bringing one graphic element to tie in print package theme, such as the seashell image from the front of the invitation. Graphics are smaller and more subtle than city-chic style, just a touch of "scenery" guests can expect.

Seasonal

Color: Depends on the season. Summers are like tropical fruits and flowers: oranges, yellows, ocean blues; springs are pastels like pink, peachy, yellows, lighter oranges, sage greens, lilacs and lavenders; falls are burnt oranges and cinnamon colors, rust reds, hunter greens; winters are reds, evergreens, silver and blue, golds and coppers, burgundies, navies.

Panel style: Single-panel, dual- or tri-fold, scroll or origami. For summer, fan invitations work.

Shape: Rectangle, square, oval, circle (works well for an informal summer invitation as a beach ball print), leaf, heart, or even Christmas tree if your wedding will be held during that time.

Graphics and borders: Colored borders to match the color of font, monogram, flourish or graphics using seasonal colors and images (such as sea horse for summer wedding, a border of daisies for a spring wedding, a border of ivy for a garden wedding, doves on snowy branches for a winter wedding). Invitations may be tied or bound with a cord in coordinating color, with a charm to match the seasonal theme of the wedding. Ribbon-tie tops for spring and summer invitations using a matching or coordinating color to the font.

Wording flair: Formal invitations stick to the formal wording rules, less formal invitations open up your freedom to personalize your wording, such as "Join us for cocktails on the terrace and dining alfresco in the cool summer evening breeze."

Personality: Celebratory, reverent of the seasons, beauty based, warm in fall and winter, showing how much you love that season

Inserts: Match or coordinate with invitation style. Additional inserts may include a printout on summer allergy info for an outdoor wedding in spring and summer (www. nasal-allergies.com), invitations to summer post-wedding pool party, even family favorite recipe for hot toddies. Guests love receiving these kinds of surprise inserts at this time.

Locational

Color: Match to your location, such as the pink sand of Bermuda mixed with the cool blue of the ocean, the deep purples of sunset in the desert, pastels and brights for a botanical garden, matching the invitation to the color of your mother's prize roses in her garden where the wedding will be held.

Panel style: Any style

Shape: Any shape

Graphics and borders: Match to color scheme; bring location into your graphics, such as palm trees or butterflies for your beach or botanical garden locale.

Wording flair: Follow traditional invitation wording, perhaps with mention not to miss the night sky in the desert, or the tulip fields during the drive to the ceremony site.

Personality: Locational pride, beauty, reverence for nature, an artistic eye toward the color of your site (which may have led you to choose it); design brings in the personality of the location.

Inserts: To match the invitation package, add additional printout of local FYIs, cultural rules, even preview lists of what guests can look forward to for your wedding weekend, or a simple note about why you chose and love this location.

Graphic Block

Color: White with black, gray or slate blue print with splash of red, or Andy Warhol–type color block invitation

Panel style: Single panel

Shape: Square or round

Graphics and borders: Matching in color style, graphics may be color-blocked or word-art curved, 3D, or other design; uses cutouts

Wording flair: Personalized, yet capturing the essentials from the traditional script

Personality: Spare, architectural, visual, contrast, artistic, "city-chic industrial" as so many nightclubs and hot spots are doing their own design.

Inserts: Matching in style to the invitation

Informal

Color: Any color you wish, from traditional white to pastels to brights, also informal papers like laser printer stationery with graphics printed on them, recycled papers with flowers or confetti embedded into them, or handwritten note cards in your choice of design or monogram letter cards.

Panel style: Single panel, dual-fold, or tri-fold

Shape: Rectangle or square are the most popular options, but you will find round or oval papers on the market.

Graphics and borders: Your choice of artistic borders and graphics to match your color scheme and location or style of the wedding

Wording flair: No need to follow the traditional rules of invitation wording unless you want to. An example of informal wording might be "John and I invite you to the wedding of our daughter Emily on Saturday, June 5th, at . . ." or a more playful "We're finally tying the knot! Join us at Pier A in Hoboken at 6 p.m. on Friday, July 4th for our ceremony and fireworks . . ."

Personality: Relaxed, informal, conversational, bright, excited

Inserts: Uusually, none. RSVP information is printed on the invitation, but you may include RSVP cards, postcards, or maps as with any other invitation style.

Destination

Color: Any range of color from whites to pastels to island tropical colors such as a mango orange or lime green, usually a seafoam blue or aquamarine, the pink of a sand beach in Bermuda, or winter whites and silvers for a winter destination wedding

Panel style: Single panel, dual- or tri-fold, scroll, origami, or booklet

Shape: Your choice. Any shape will do.

Graphics and borders: Color-matched to the print hue, or a border of destination theme shapes like seashells or garden vines. Digital camera graphics might include a shot of the two of you on vacation, on the beach, by an ocean sunset to convey the mood.

Wording flair: The traditional script is altered with reference to the location, such as "Join us in the Bahamas for . . ."

Personality: Exotic, excited, colorful, escapist, sun-bright, transporting, conversational

Inserts: Details on flights and lodging, itineraries for weekend events, details on passports and IDs, a link to your personalized wedding website for more details and travel arrangements

Cultural

Color: The colors of your culture, such as the oranges, reds, and yellows of Morocco

Panel style: Any style

Shape: Any shape

Graphics and borders: Include colored borders and graphics to convey the cultural style of your celebration. Be sure to avoid cliché, though. The sombrero probably isn't your best bet, so go with patterns and colors rather than typical graphics.

Wording flair: Formal invitation wording works to match your formal wedding, or informal wording to match your informal style. You can print some invitations in the native language of some of your relatives, or do dual-language invites with English on one side and, say, Spanish on the other.

Personality: Pride in your heritage, excitement, honoring relatives and family tradition

Inserts: Traditional inserts as needed

Font Style

In years past, brides and grooms were offered a half dozen types of print styles (called *fonts*). Now, artistry has turned fonts into a sprawling world of creativity. Old World etiquette required the "proper" use of a single italic font with the warning to be sure all letters are legible, and it was considered revolutionary when invitation designers allowed bridal couples to use two different fonts on the same invitation.

STYLE NOTES FROM DOMINIQUE

A great way to draw attention when two fonts are used on the same invitation is to utilize two different, coordinating ink colors as well. This simple enhancement creates a fresh, updated look.
—Dominique Schurman, Papyrus

Now, from ultraformal to informal invitations and print items, your choice of fonts are as varied as your choice of wedding gowns and cakes. You can go traditional with italic prints, blocky with square fonts, playful with rounded prints, even choose from a range of handwriting fonts to make it look like you wrote out each of your invitations by hand. Patty Brahe of mountaincow. com shares a chart of their Printing Press Weddings fonts to give you an idea of the style elements available today. As you review them, be mindful of the descriptions that come to mind: elegant, natural, flirty, exotic, and so on. The right font will jump out at you, and we encourage you to play with different fonts to determine your style.

- -

FONT STYLES FROM PATTY BRAHE OF MOUNTAINCOW.COM
Use this chart to find inspiration to create your ideal wedding stationery:

If your wedding style is . . .	*You'll love these fonts . . .*	*Consider these colors . . .*	*Keep in mind . . .*
Traditional Bridal Formal	**Alyssa Noodles**	**Ivory, Café au Lait (ivory and chocolate brown)**	**Add a twist to traditional by changing your margins, using lower-case letters, or substituting black or gray text with brown or red.**

If your wedding style is . . .	*You'll love these fonts . . .*	*Consider these colors . . .*	*Keep in mind . . .*
Modern Elegance	**Alyssa Afternoon**	**Evening Sky (twilight and midnight blues)**	**Two-tone invitations are a great way to set a color scheme and add weight to a DIY invitation**
Handwriting	**Meegles**	**Cotton Candy (greens and pinks)**	**Use handwriting or very stylized fonts for your less formal invitation pieces like shower invitations.**
Old World Calligraphy	**Isabelle Alyssa Black Tie**	**Ivory/ deep red**	**Swoopy, script fonts are beautiful, but the most important function of a font is to be readable. Combine it with a block font when sending out important information.**
Trendy	**Beckles**	**Strawberry Truffle (brown and pink)**	**Add dark pink envelope liners to ivory stationery for a shot of color.**
Feminine	**SkyPie**	**Bubblegum (mixing shades of pink)**	**Use scalloped-edge paper for an extra girlie flair that's perfect for bridal showers.**

If your wedding style is . . .	You'll love these fonts . . .	Consider these colors . . .	Keep in mind . . .
Flirty (bachelorette (parties)	**Beckles**	**Rock Candy (blues and greens)**	**Find bridesmaids that look just like your girlfriends on mountaincow.com's Fonts and Graphics for Weddings.**
Playful and Funky	**Ryan**	**Avocado**	**Use all lower case—even on your envelopes.**
Tropical (island and beach	**Beckles Wide**	**Warm combo (oranges and whites) for tropics and Cool combo (blues and greens) for beach**	**Don't stick with one color, mix different shades for a beautiful spectrum.**
Bold	**Benjamin Caps**	**Pistachio and brown**	**Mix scripts with block letters, print a dark block of color to contrast with light colored text.**
Clean, Minimalist	**Jackson Junior Sans, circle monogram**	**Midnight (white or ivory with navy blue)**	**Create a married monogram for the stationery you'll use after the wedding.**

Wording

Beyond your design style, the wording of your invitation will convey the style of your wedding as a whole. Formal wording tells your guests that this will be a formal wedding, and that they should dress appropriately. Informal wording about your sunset beach celebration tells guests what to expect. There's also a big collection of etiquette rules when it comes to invitation wording, so be sure to look at the examples on such sites as www. weddingchannel.com, www.weddingsolutions.com, www.theknot .com, and the sites for your favorite bridal magazines. You'll find wording advice on the top situations (such as divorced parents hosting), or you can even submit your own particular wording questions for personalized answers at www.sharonnaylor.net.

Inserts

The most common and traditional inserts that you'll see offered as part of invitation packages are reception cards, response cards, maps, and sometimes separate menu choice cards. As you've seen in the previous examples, these cards will be created to match or complement your invitation design. You *can* add a single monogram, logo, or delicate graphic to your response cards if the color and style complements what you have on your invitations. Consider your invitation style and make notes here on how you'll tie your style into these little inserts. Will you print a smaller version of your monogram or logo? Add the same color ribbon you have on your invitation? Design your print style in your Possibilities Notebook.

Wedding Programs

For your wedding program, your style is just as important as your substance. When wedding guests arrive at the ceremony, they'll be handed your program—and it's one of the first beautiful expressions of your style that they'll see on your Big Day. It sets the tone, connotes the personality of your ceremony, delivers a message. First impressions last, and your program is their introduction to the story you will tell with every element of your wedding and reception to come.

What is your wedding program style? Check off the options that appeal to you:

_____ Traditional folded rectangular

_____ Single panel rectangular

_____ Folded square

_____ Single-panel square

_____ Booklet, featuring individual pages for your bridal party names, the steps of your ceremony, a note from you, and so on

_____ Program printed on a fan

_____ Scroll

Your program color should match the colors of your wedding, but you can go neutral with an off-white or white, printed with your logo or monogram, or even your photo on the front cover. Most couples design their own, so record your style notes in your Possibilities Notebook.

NOTE FROM THE AUTHORS

Thank you for allowing us to help you define your wedding style! Often, it's just a matter of asking questions with a focus on your love story that gets you to converge your two separate styles into the perfect blend for your wedding day. Your wedding is a once-in-a-lifetime reflection of your relationship, your history, your culture, your beliefs, your love story. Completing this process is cause for celebration!

You've done the detailed work that so many couples skip in a passive approach to "just get it done" or have someone else tell them what's going to "work" for their setting. From engagement party to after-party, you've done yourselves a great honor in paying tribute to each other's visions and bringing a great level of play to your wedding plans.

We hope you'll continue to use this book in the future when it's time to discover your new home's style, your nursery style, your entertaining style, and more.

It's also our hope that you've learned a little bit more about each other, that you've enjoyed this process, and that you will share with us the wonderful story of your Big Day. We'd love to include you in future editions of this book, as well as on our websites. So please do contact us through www.sharonnaylor.net and www.botanicalschicago.com. Let us hear from you!

ALL THE BEST,
SHARON NAYLOR AND CASEY COOPER

Idea Dream Sheet

Use this space to record your inspirations, notes, and ideas as you go along. . . . The words you write here could springboard a theme or a décor idea, the perfect description to show to your wedding experts.

_____

_____

_____

_____

_____

_____

_____

_____

_____

_____

_____

_____

_____

_____

_____

_____

Idea Dream Sheet

Resources

This list is purely for your research use, and does not imply endorsement or recommendation of the companies or products. Since websites change over the course of time, we apologize if any Web addresses are no longer accessible.

Wedding Planning Websites

Bliss Weddings: www.blissweddings.com
Bridal Guide: www.bridalguide.com
Brides: www.brides.com
Hitch New York: www.hitchny.com
The Knot: www.theknot.com
Martha Stewart Weddings: www.marthastewart.com
Pash Weddings: www.pashweddings.com
Town and Country Weddings: www.townandcountry.com
Wedding Channel: www.weddingchannel.com
Wedding Solutions: www.weddingsolutions.com

Gowns

After Six Men's Formalwear & Tuxedos
    www.aftersix.com; info@aftersix.com
    Collins Industrial Boulevard, Athens, GA 30603-1647

Alfred Angelo
    www.alfredangelo.com; info@alfredangelo.com
    1690 South Congress Avenue, Suite 120, Delray Beach, FL 33445
    800-528-3589, 866–8angelo [826-4356] (stores)
    877-7angelo [726-4356] (appointments)

Bill Levkoff, Inc.
    www.billlevkoff.com; questions@billlevkoff.com
    8 Westchester Plaza, Elmsford, NY 10523

Bloomingdales.com
    www.bloomingdales.com
    P.O. Box 8215, Mason, OH 45040
    866-593-2540

David's Bridal
    www.davidsbridal.com
    877-923-BRIDE [2743] (appointments)

The Dessy Group
    www.dessy.com

JCPenney, Corp.
    www.jcpenney.com
    P.O. Box 10001, Dallas, TX 75301-7311
    Attn: Corp Customer Relations
    800-322-1189

Jessica McClintock, Inc.
    Corporate headquarters
    www.jessicamcclintock.com
    customer_service@jessicamcclintock.com
    1400 16th Street, San Francisco, CA 94103
    800-711-8718

Jim Hjelm Occasions/JLM Couture
    www.jimhjelmoccasions.com
    525 7th Avenue, Suite 1703, New York, NY 10018

Macy's
  Corporate headquarters
  www.macys.com
  151 West 34th Street, New York, NY 10001; 800-289-6229

Melissa Sweet
  www.melissasweet.com
  800-970-9205

Mori Lee
  www.morilee.com

Spiegel
  www.spiegel.com
  800-222-5680 (customer service); 800-345-4500 (orders)

Vera Wang Corporate
  www.verawang.com
  225 West 39th Street, 9th Floor, New York, NY 10018
  212-575-6400

Vera Wang Flagship Salon
  www.verawang.com
  991 Madison Avenue, New York, NY 10021
  212-628-3400

Vera Wang Maids on Madison
  www.verawang.com
  980 Madison Avenue, New York, NY 10021
  212-628-9898

Watters and Watters
  www.watters.com

Shoes and Accessories

David's Bridal
   www.davidsbridal.com
   877-923-BRIDE [2743] (appointments)

Dyeables
   www.dyeables.com; customer_service@dyeables.com

Fenaroli for Regalia Fenaroli
   www.fenaroli.com; contactus@fenaroli.com
   311 Summer Street, 1st Floor, Rear, Boston, MA 02210
   617-350-6556

JCPenney, Corp.
   www.jcpenney.com
   Attn: Corporate Customer Relations
   P.O. Box 10001, Dallas, TX 75301-7311
   800-322-1189

Kenneth Cole
   www.kennethcole.com
   800-KEN-COLE [536-2653]

Laura Lee Designs
   www.lauraleedesigns.com; info@LauraLeeDesigns.com
   888-553-2247

My Little Pretty
   www.mylittlepretty.com; kristy@mylittlepretty.com

Nina Footwear
   www.ninashoes.com; info@ninashoes.com
   800-281-9742

Salon Shoes
    www.salonshoes.com; info@salonshoes.com

Steve Madden
    www.stevemadden.com; info@stevemaddendirect.com
    888-smadden [762–3336] (USA); 703-637-0022 (International)

The Pearl Outlet
    www.thepearloutlet.com; info@thepearloutlet.com (general)
    sales@thepearloutlet.com (sales)
    support@thepearloutlet.com (customer support)
    3191 Green Mountain Road, Kalama, WA 98625
    866-673-3036 (USA); 360-673-3043 (International)

Watters & Watters
    www.watters.com

Beauty

Avon
    www.avon.com
    1345 Avenue of the Americas, New York, NY 10020
    212-282-5000

Beauty On Call
    www.beautyoncall.com; stacey@beautyoncall.com
    1323 North Mohawk, Chicago, IL 60610, Attn: Stacey Koerner
    312-335-5350

Bobbi Brown Essentials
    www.bobbibrown.com
    877-310-9222

Carefair LTD
   www.carefair.com
   Chamerstrasse 12c, Zug 6304 Switzerland
   011-41-5163010059 (when calling from USA)

Clinique Laboratories, LLC
   www.clinique.com
   corporate headquarters: 767 5th Avenue, New York, NY 10153
   212-572-3800

Elizabeth Arden
   www.elizabetharden.com; consumer@elizabetharden.com
   EA Consumer Affairs, 309 South Street, New Providence, NJ 07974
   866-217-2927 (customer service); 800-326-7337 (consumer affairs)

Estee Lauder, Inc.
   www.esteelauder.com
   corporate headquarters: 767 5th Avenue, New York, NY 10153
   877-311-3883

The Gal Pals
   www.thegalpals.com; admin@thegalpals.com
   (formerly: iBeauty)

Lancôme, USA
   www.lancome.com
   corporate headquarters: 575 5th Avenue, New York, NY 10017
   800-LANCOME [526-2663]

L'Oreal USA, Inc.
   www.loreal.com
   corporate headquarters: 575 5th Avenue, New York, NY 10017
   212-818-1500

Mac
  www.maccosmetics.com
  800-387-6707

Makeover Studio/Clairol
  www.makeoverstudio.com
  Clairol, Inc., World Headquarters, 1 Blachley Road,
  Stamford, CT 06922
  800-252-4765 (customer service, "try it on" studio)

Max Factor
  www.maxfactor.com

Maybelline
  www.maybelline.com
  800-944-0730

Neutrogena
  www.neutrogena.com
  800-582-4048

Pantene
  www.pantene.com

Rembrandt
  www.rembrandt.com

Revlon
  www.revlon.com
  800-473-8566

Sephora USA, Inc.
  www.sephora.com
  First Market Tower, 525 Market Street, 11th Floor,
  San Francisco, CA 94105–2708
  877-737-4672

Jewelry

A Diamond Is Forever
  www.adiamondisforever.com
  (Information source on diamonds)

American Gem Society
  www.ags.org
  8881 W. Sahara Avenue, Las Vegas, NV 89117
  866-805-6500

Aurum Design Jewelry
  www.aurumdesign.com; sales@aurumdesign.com
  116 West 4th Street, Rochester, MI 48307
  248-651-9040

Blue Nile
  www.bluenile.com; service@bluenile.com (US)
  service@bluenile.ca (Canada)
  800-242-2728 (US); 888-565-7609 (Canada); 0 808 234-7461 (UK)

Cartier
  www.cartier.com
  800-227-8437

Diamond.com, USA
  www.diamond.com
  1083 Main Street, Champlain, NY 12919
  888-DIAMOND [342-6663]

Diamond.com, Canada
www.diamond.com
4058 Jean Talon W., Suite 200, Montreal, Quebec H4P 1V5
877-602-3817

Diamond Cutters International
www.diamondcuttersintl.com
800-275-4047 (helpline)

Hearts on Fire
www.heartsonfire.com

Ice.com, USA
www.ice.com
1083 Main Street, Champlain, NY 12919
800-539-3580 (US)

Ice.com, Canada
www.ice.com
4058 Jean Talon W., Suite 200, Montreal, QC. H4P 1V5
800-539-3580 (Canada)

Jewelry Information Center
www.jic.org; info@jic.org
52 Vanderbilt Avenue, 19th Floor, New York, NY 10017
646-658-0240 (NY), 800-459-0130 (US)

Jewelry.com
www.jewelry.com; help@jewelry.com
609 Greenwich Street, 3rd Floor, New York, NY 10014

My Little Pretty
www.mylittlepretty.com; kristy@mylittlepretty.com

Paul Klecka, Inc.
    www.klecka.com; info@klecka.com
    13553 Poway Road, Suite 336, Poway, CA 92064
    858-380-6767

The Pearl Outlet
    www.thepearloutlet.com; info@thepearloutlet.com (general)
    sales@thepearloutlet.com (sales)
    support@thepearloutlet.com (customer support)
    3191 Green Mountain Road, Kalama, WA 98625
    866-673-3036 (USA); 360-673-3043 (International)

Tiffany & Co.
    www.tiffany.com
    800-843-3269

Zales
    www.zales.com
    800-311-5393

Invitations

Aurum Design
    www.aurum-design.com; neille@aurum-design.com
    7604 Harwood Avenue, Milwaukee, WI 53213
    414-777-0015

An Invitation to Buy Nationwide
    www.invitations4sale.com; Linda@invitations4sale.com
    708-203-4449

Anna Griffin, Inc.
> www.annagriffin.com; info@annagriffin.com
> 2270 Marietta Boulevard, Atlanta, GA 30318
> 888-817-8170

Botanical PaperWorks
> www.botanicalpaperworks.com; info@botanicalpaperworks.com
> 877-956-7393

Crane & Co., Inc. (World Headquarters)
> www.crane.com; customerservice@crane.com
> 30 South Street, Dalton, MA 01226
> 800-268-2281

Evangel Christian Invitations Available through
> Ann's Bridal Bargains
> www.annsbridalbargains.com; service@annsbridalbargains.com
> 800-821-7011

Invite Site
> www.invitesite.com; helen@invitesite.com
> (made from recycled paper) scott@invitesite.com
> 888-349-468

Mountaincow
> www.mountaincow.com; judith@mountaincow.com
> Software Products & Materials, see "Gallery" on website *Online Only*
> 800-797-MCOW [6269]

PaperStyle.com, Inc.
> www.paperstyle.com
> 11390 Old Roswell Road, Suite 122, Alpharetta, GA 30004
> 888-670-5300, ext.4

Papyrus Online.com
   www.papyrusonline.com; customerservice@papyrusonline.com
   Customer Service, 500 Chadbourne Road, Box 6030, Fairfield, CA
   94533

Precious Collection
   www.preciouscollection.com; 38Precious@preciouscollection.com
   877-761-8508

PSA Essentials
   www.psaessentials.com; sales@psaessentials.com
   1239 Anderson, Clawson, MI 48017
   800-537-5222, 248-288-7584

Vismara Invitations
   www.vismarainvitations.com; inquiries@VismaraInvitations.com
   retail@Vismaralvitations.com
   746 Fox Street, Denver, CO 80204
   303-378-4921

You're Invited
   www.youreinvited.com; info@youreinvited.com
   2 Main Drive, Brookfield, CT 06804
   877-468-4834, 203-790-0680

Calligraphy

Calligraphy by Kristen
   www.calligraphybykristen

Petals and Ink
   www.petalsnink.com
   818-509-6783

Linens

BBJ Linen
  www.bbjlinen.com
  Corporate Office, 7855 Gross Point Road, Skokie, IL 60077
  800-260-1030; 847-329-8400

Carousel
  www.carousellinen.com
  454 Sheridan Road, Highwood, IL 60040
  847-432-8182; 800-238-8182

Chair Covers Online
  www.chaircoversonline.com
  Chair Covers & Linens, 25914 John R. Road,
  Madison Heights, MI 48071
  800-260-1030; 248-548-5600

Resource One
  www.resourceone.info
  818-343-3451 (Los Angeles); 212-255-0855 (New York)

Live Butterflies

Butterfly Celebration
  www.butterflycelebration.com; celebration@insectlore.com (US)
  insect@insectlore.co.uk (Europe)
  800-548-3284

Swallowtail Farms, Inc.
  www.swallowtailfarms.com; info@swallowtailfarms.com
  P.O. Box 4737, El Dorado Hills, CA 95762
  888-441-2041

Music and Entertainment

Amazon.com
  www.amazon.com

Barnes & Noble
  www.bn.com
  800-843-2665 (US); 201-272-3651 (International)

Fig Media
  www.figmediainc.com
  1120 West Granville Avenue, Chicago, IL 60660
  773-338-1334

Lyrics Depot
  www.lyricsdepot.com

Lyrics Freak
  www.lyricsfreak.com

Music in the Air
  www.musicintheair.com; musicintheair@aol.com
  212-946-1563 (New York area)

Rank Entertainment
  www.rankentertainment.com
  2133 West Le Moyne, Chicago, IL 60622
  773-489-6047

Piano Brothers
  www.pianobrothers.com
  The O'Neill Brothers, 111 West Main Street,
  New Prague, MN 56071
  888-966-3455; 952-758-9300

Romantic Lyrics
www.romanticlyrics.com

Sing 365
www.sing365.com

Wedding Channel
www.weddingchannel.com
888-989-9333

Limousines

National Limousine Association
www.limo.org
patricia.nelson@limo.org (Executive Director)
darcie.benard@limo.org (Member Services Coordinator)
49 South Maple Avenue, Marlton, NJ 08053
800-652-7007

Flowers

Ariella Flowers
www.ariellaflowers.com; ariellachezar@mindspring.com
518-584-8798

Botanicals, Inc.
www.botanicalschicago.com
2214 North Elston Avenue, Chicago, IL 60614
773–269–3142

Floral Design Institute
www.floraldesigninstitute.com
Questions@FloralDesignInstitute.com
800–819–8089

HGTV
  www.hgtv.com
  865-694-7879

Daniel Ost
  www.danielost.be
  9100 Sint-Niklass, Belgium
  32-3-776-17-15

Preston Bailey
  www.prestonbailey.com
  147 West 25th Street, New York, NY 10001
  212-741-9300

The Velvet Garden
  www.thevelvetgarden.com
  8327 West Third Street, Los Angeles, CA 90048
  323-852-1766

Art Fool
  www.artfool.com
  161 Allen Street, New York, NY 10002
  212-253-2737

David Beahm Design
  www.davidbeahm.com
  212-947-1801

Sierra Flower Finder
  www.sierraflowerfinder.com
  514-733-3515 (Montreal)

Favors

MoMA Store
  www.momastore.com; orderservices@moma.org
  800-793-3167

My Wedding Labels
  www.myweddinglabels.com
  888-412-5636

The Pajama Gram Company
  www.pajamagram.com
  6655 Shelbourne Road, Shelbourne, VT 05482
  Attn: Customer Service
  888-518-2327

Pearl River (Asian)
  www.pearlriver.com; pearlriver@pearlriver.com
  800-878-2446

Pepper People
  www.pepperpeople.com

Pier 1
  www.pier1.com
  800-245-4595

Surfas (gourmet food)
  www.surfasonline.com; Customerservice@surfasonline.com
  8824 National Boulevard, Culver City, CA 90232
  866-799-4770, 310-559-477

Wedding Things
 www.weddingthings.com; info@weddingthings.com
 #118-408 East Kent Avenue South, Vancouver, BC V5X 4N6
   Canada
 888-338-8818 (US & Canada)

Gourmet Food

Ben & Jerry's: www.benjerry.com
 Ben & Jerry's Homemade, Inc., 30 Community Drive,
 South Burlington, VT 05403–6828
 802–846–1500

Cheryl & Co.: www.cherylandco.com; 800–367–2715

Drink Gus: www.drinkgus.com
 212–355–7454; info@drinkgus.com

Utmost Brands, Inc.
 424 East 57th Street, Suite 3C, New York, NY 10022

Fizzy Lizzy, LLC
 www.fizzylizzy.com; liz@fizzylizzy.com
 265 Lafayette Street, Suite D20, New York, NY 10012
 800-203-9336

Gail Watson Custom Cakes
 www.gailwatsoncakes.com; gail@gailwatsoncake.com
 335 West 38th Street, Suite 11, New York, NY 10018
 877-867-5088

Izze Beverage Co.
 www.izze.com; robin.allin@izze.com (Div. & Reg. Sales)
 kristen.crown@izze.com (National Sales)

david.britton@izze.com (International Sales)
2990 Center Green Court South, Boulder, CO 80301
303-327-5515; 303-327-5515

M&M's
www.mms.com
800-627-7852

Park Avenue Club
www.parkavenueclub.com; catering@parkavenueclub.com
973-301-8233

Personal Chef Association
www.personalchef.com; info@personalchef.com
800-644-8389

American Personal & Private Chef Association
4572 Delaware Street, San Diego, CA 92116

Ron Ben-Israel Wedding Cakes
www.weddingcakes.com

Surfas Restaurant & Supply
www.surfasonline.com; customerservice@surfasonline.com
8824 National Boulevard, Culver City, CA 90232
866-799-4770; 310-559-4770

Steazsoda
www.steazsoda.com; info@steaz.com
800-295-1388

The Healthy Beverage Co.
  2865 South Eagle Road, MB 356, Newton, PA 18940

Wilton Industries
  www.wilton.com; info@wilton.com
  2240 West 75th Street, Woodridge, IL 60517
  800-794-5866; 630-963-1818

The Food Network
  www.foodtv.com

Zingerman's
  www.zingermans.com; toni@zingermans.com
  422 Detroit Street, Ann Arbor, MI 48104
  888-636-8162

Wine and Champagne

Wine.com
  www.wine.com

Wine Searcher
  www.winesearcher.com
  P.O. Box 41463, St. Luke, 3 Gordon Road,
  Auckland, New Zealand 1346

Wine Spectator
  www.winespectator.com

Caterers and Chefs

International Associations of Culinary Professionals
www.iacp.com; iacp@hqtrs.com
304 West Liberty Street, Suite 201, Louisville, KY 40202
800-928-4227, 502-581-9786

International Special Events Society
www.ises.com; info@ises.com
401 North Michigan Avenue, Chicago, IL 60611-4267
800-688-4737, 312-321-6853

Limelight Catering
www.limelightcatering.com; inquiry@limelightcatering.com
2000 North Racine Avenue, Chicago, IL 60614
773-883-3080

National Association of Catering Executives
www.nace.net
NACE Headquarters, 9881 Broken Land Parkway, Suite 101,
Columbia, MD 21046
410-290-5410

Personal Chef Association
www.personalchef.com; info@personalchef.com
800-644-8389

American Personal & Private Chef Association
4572 Delaware Street, San Diego, CA 92116

Rentals

American Rental Association
  www.ararental.org
  1900 19th Street, Moline, IL 61265
  800-334-2177

Halls Rental
  www.hallsrental.com
  6130 West Howard, Niles, IL 60714
  847-929-2222

Tablescapes, Ltd.
  www.tablescapes.com
  1827 West Hubbard Street, Chicago, IL 60622-6236
  312-733-9700

Warehouse Stores

BJ's Wholesale Club
  www.bjs.com

Costco: www.costco.com;
  P.O. Box 34331, Seattle, WA 98124
  800–774–2678 (general member services)

Sam's Club: www.samsclub.com

Crafts and Paper

Flax Art
  www.flaxart.com; askus@flaxart.com
  800-343-3529

Michaels Stores, Inc.
   www.michaels.com
   Attn: Customer Service, 8000 Bent Branch Drive, Irving, TX 75063
   800-642-4235

My Wedding Labels
   www.myweddinglabels.com
   888-412-5636

Office Max
   www.officemax.com
   800-283-7674

Paper Access
   www.paperaccess.com; info@PaperPresentation.com (contact
   PaperPresentation.com)
   800-727-3701

Paper Direct
   www.paperdirect.com
   800-272-7377

Papersource
   www.paper-source.com
   800-PAPER-11 [727-3711]

Papyrus
   www.papyrusonline.com

Scrapjazz
   www.scrapjazz.com
   116 North Lindsay Road, Suite 4, Mesa, AZ 85213

Online Invitations

BlueMountain Arts
    www.bluemountain.com; BlueMountain.com
    Customer Service, One American Road, Cleveland, OH 44144

Evite
    www.evite.com

Hallmark
    www.hallmark.com

Photo Albums

Adesso Albums
    www.adessoalbums.com; questions@adessoalbums.com
    665 Third Street, Suite 521, San Francisco, CA 94107
    415-957-9901

Exposures
    www.exposuresonline.com; csr@exposuresonline.com
    1 Memory Lane, P.O. Box 3615, Oshkosh, WI 54903–3615
    800-222-4947 (orders); 800-572-5750 (customer service)

Travel

Amtrak
    www.amtrak.com
    800-872-7245

ATMS Travel News (Adventure Gateways)
    www.atmstravelnews.com
    970-568-7423

Adventure Travel Media Source
   6936 Raleigh Street, Wellington, CO 80549

Charmed Places
   www.charmedplaces.com; tammy@charmedplaces.com
   P.O. Box 669, Stone Ridge, NY 12484
   845-658-9077

Couples Resorts
   www.couples.com
   11902 Miramar Parkway, Miramar, FL 33025
   800-268-7537

Expedia
   www.expedia.com

Hilton
   www.hilton.com
   800-774-1500 (Canada & US)

Ibero Star
   www.iberostar.com

Occidental
   www.occidentalhotels.com
   800-858-2258

Palace Resorts
   www.palaceresorts.com
   8725 NW 18th Terrace, Suite 301, Miami, FL 33172
   800-635-1836; 800-346-8225

Porthole Magazine
www.porthole.com; bpanoff@ppigroup.com

Sandals
www.sandals.com
888-sandals [726-3257]

Super Clubs
www.superclubs.com; info@superclubs.com
Attn: Customer Service, 2021 Hayes Street, Hollywood, FL 33020
877-467-8737

Tourism Offices Worldwide Directory
www.towd.com

Travel and Leisure Magazine
www.travelandleisure.com
800-888-8728

Travelocity
www.travelocity.com

Travelzoo
www.travelzoo.com

VRBO
www.vrbo.com; webmaster@vrbo.com

VRBO.Com, Inc.
3801 South Capital of Texas Highway, Suite 150,
Austin, TX 78704

Bed-and-Breakfasts

Bed & Breakfast Inns Online
  www.bbonline.com
  909 North Sepulveda Boulevard, 11th Floor, El Segundo, CA 90245
  800-215-7365

bnbfinder.com
  www.bnbfinder.com; 888-547-8226

Bed & Breakfast List
  www.bnblist.com; info@bnblist.com

The Inn Keeper.com
  www.theinnkeeper.com; sales@theinnkeeper.com
  comments@theinnkeeper.com
  P.O. Box 1615, Venice, FL 34284
  800-582-1643 (US), 207-582-8256 (outside US)

Vacation Spot.com
  www.vacationspot.com
  888-219-7786 (US & Canada); 817-377-1353 (worldwide)
  888-903-7768 (book by phone)

Special Event Associations

The Association of Bridal Consultants
  www.bridalassn.com; office@bridalassn.com
  56 Danbury Road, Suite 11, New Milford, CT 06776
  860-355-0464

International Special Event Society
  www.ises.com; info@ises.com
  800-688-4737; 312-321-6853

ISES
  401 North Michigan Avenue, Chicago, IL 60611-4267

NJWedding.com
  www.njwedding.com; info@njwedding.com
  Wedding & Event Business Resource Center
  c/o Kent Enterprises, LLC, 15 Hendrickson Drive,
  Belle Mead, NJ 08502
  908-874-0417

Professional Photographers of America
  www.ppa.com
  229 Peach Tree Street NE, Suite 2200, Atlanta, GA 30303
  800-786-6277, 404-533-8600

Wedding & Portrait Photographers Intl.
  www.eventphotographers.com
  P.O. Box 2003, 1312 Lincoln Boulevard, Santa Monica,
    CA 90406-2003
  301-451-0090

Wedding & Event Videographers Association International
  www.weva.com

Wedding Officiants.com: www.weddingofficiants.com
  paul@weddingofficiants.com

Weather and Sunset

Allergy Tracker
  www.nasal-allergies.com

Astronomical Applications Department
  help@aa.usno.navy.mil; aa.usno.navy.mil
  U.S. Naval Observatory, 3450 Massachusetts Avenue NW,
  Washington, DC 20392-5420
  202-762-1617

The Weather Channel
  www.weatherchannel.com

Wedding Coordinators

Preston Bailey
  www.prestonbailey.com; info@prestonbailey.com
  212-741-9300

Birch Design Studio
  www.birchdesign.com
  614 9th Avenue NE, Calgary, AB T2E 0W3, Canada
  403-273-5253

Bliss! Weddings
  www.blissweddings.com
  P.O. Box 363, Woodbury, NY 11797-9998

Colin Cowie
  www.ColinCowie.com

Frank Event Design
  www.frankeventdesign.com
  5555 North Sheridan Road, Arcade Level, Chicago, IL 60640
  773-275-6804

Randie Pellegrini
   www.cordiallyinvited.com; rwp@cordiallyinvited.com
   800-507-7505

Sasha Souza
   www.sashasouzaevents.com
   707-253-8160 (Napa); 310-860-7428 (Southern California)

Additional Sites of Interest

Bayley's Boxes
   www.bayleysboxes.com; sales@bayleysboxes.com

Brainy Quotes
   www.brainyquotes.com

Color Wheel
   www.sessions.edu/ilu
   800-258-4115, ext. 7 (from US), 212-239-3080, ext. 11

Cost of Wedding
   www.costofwedding.com

Courtship Stories
   www.courtship-stories.com
   888-427-8584; 909-499-3429

Frost Lighting
   www.frostlighting.com

Personal Stamps
   www.photostamps.com

Photo Stamps at Stamps.com
  12959 Coral Tree Place, Los Angeles, CA 90066-7020

TableWareToday.com
  www.tablewaretoday.com

The Wedding Report
  www.theweddingreport.com

Wedding Details
  www.weddingdetails.com; linda@weddingdetails.com
  10850 Traverse Highway, Suite 1010, Traverse City, MI 49684
  888-968-5565

The Wedding Goddess
  www.weddinggoddess.com; RevLaurieSue@weddinggoddess.com

Index